VICTIMS' EXPERIENCES OF THE CRIMINAL JUSTICE RESPONSE TO DOMESTIC ABUSE

FEMINIST DEVELOPMENTS IN VIOLENCE AND ABUSE

Series Editors: Dr Hannah Bows, Durham University (UK) and Professor Nicole Westmarland, Durham University (UK)

Feminist Developments in Violence and Abuse provides a feminist forum for academic work that pushes forward existing knowledge around violence and abuse, informing policy and practice, with the overarching objective of contributing towards ending violence and abuse within our society. The series enables academics, practitioners, policymakers and professionals to continually build and explore their understanding of the dynamics, from the micro to the macro level, that are driving violence and abuse. The study of abuse and violence has a large scope for co-producing research, and this series is a home for research involving a broad range of stakeholders, particularly those working in grassroots domestic and sexual violence organisations, police, prosecutors, lawyers, campaign groups, housing and victim services. As violence and abuse research reaches across disciplinary boundaries, the series has an interdisciplinary scope with research impact at the heart.

Available Volumes:

Victims' Experiences of the Criminal Justice Response to Domestic Abuse: Beyond Glass Walls
Emma Forbes

Forthcoming Volumes:

Understanding and Responding to Economic Abuse
Nicola Sharp-Jeffs

'Rough Sex' and the Criminal Law: Global Perspectives
Hannah Bows and Jonathan Herring

Rape Myths: Causes, Effects, and Societal Contexts
Sofia Persson and Katie Dhingra

Not Your Usual Suspect: Older Offenders of Violence and Abuse
Hannah Bows

Gendered Justice? How Women's Attempts to Cope With, Survive, or Escape Domestic Abuse Can Drive Them into Crime
Jo Roberts

VICTIMS' EXPERIENCES OF THE CRIMINAL JUSTICE RESPONSE TO DOMESTIC ABUSE

Beyond GlassWalls

BY
EMMA FORBES
University of Glasgow, United Kingdom

United Kingdom – North America – Japan – India
Malaysia – China

Emerald Publishing Limited
Howard House, Wagon Lane, Bingley BD16 1WA, UK

First edition 2022

Copyright © 2022 Emma Forbes.

Published under an exclusive license by Emerald Publishing Limited.

The author will be donating all proceeds from royalties on this book to the Daisy Project.

Reprints and permissions service
Contact: permissions@emeraldinsight.com

No part of this book may be reproduced, stored in a retrieval system, transmitted in any form or by any means electronic, mechanical, photocopying, recording or otherwise without either the prior written permission of the publisher or a licence permitting restricted copying issued in the UK by The Copyright Licensing Agency and in the USA by The Copyright Clearance Center. No responsibility is accepted for the accuracy of information contained in the text, illustrations or advertisements. The opinions expressed in these chapters are not necessarily those of the Author or the publisher.

British Library Cataloguing in Publication Data
A catalogue record for this book is available from the British Library

ISBN: 978-1-80117-389-6 (Print)
ISBN: 978-1-80117-386-5 (Online)
ISBN: 978-1-80117-388-9 (Epub)

INVESTOR IN PEOPLE

For my dad Charlie and his GlassWalls' angels ....

And for my mum, who taught us both all the
most important things.
With love

CONTENTS

Acknowledgements ix
Foreword by Lord Hope of Craighead, KT xi

Introduction 1

Chapter One The Policy Approach 15

Chapter Two Law 45

Chapter Three The Victim Experience Before Court 73

Chapter Four At Court 99

Chapter Five After Court 123

Chapter Six Improving the Justice Response 147

Chapter Seven Conclusion 173

References 183
Index 215

ACKNOWLEDGEMENTS

This book is based on doctoral research at the University of Glasgow with scholarship funding from the College of Social and Political Sciences. Thanks go to the wonderful women I was lucky to have as supervisors, Professor Michele Burman and Dr Oona Brooks-Hay.

The timeline relied upon to write Chapters One and Two was adapted as an interactive online resource as part of a Scottish Justice Fellowship, funded by Scottish Government, Scottish Centre for Crime and Justice Research (SCCJR) and Scottish Institute for Policing (SIPR). Additional funding was provided by the Clark Foundation for Legal Education. I am fortunate to have the support of SCCJR, and they have continued to provide encouragement, despite my return to prosecution practice post PhD. I am grateful to Crown Office and Procurator Fiscal Service for their support throughout the original research. It is an honour to have Lord Hope, a veteran of both jurisdictions and the bench-mark of sound judgement, write the Foreword.

At the heart of this book lies the stories of ordinary women who have faced inordinate challenges and achieved extraordinary things. As one of the research participants told me, 'I used to see stained glass in churches and wonder who made it. Now I look at it and think, I can do that'. I am so grateful for all I have learned from them. Thanks to Scottish Women's Aid, the Daisy Project, ASSIST advocacy service and all the amazing women who shared their experiences with me. The beautiful images between the chapters of this book are reproduced with kind permission from Brian Waugh, artist and sympathetically photographed by Ian Marshall. The photograph at the start of chapter 7 is reproduced with kind permission from Colin Mearns of *The Herald* and *The Evening Times*.

This is the first time I have written a book and juggling it with full-time work in a pandemic was a stretch. Thanks to Professors Nicole Westmarland and Hannah Bows for having faith in my pitch and to Katy Mathers, Kirsty Woods and the fantastic team at Emerald for their patient guidance through the process.

I'm grateful to Gillian Baker for helpful chats on the civil process and to Peter Reid (University of Glasgow, PhD forthcoming) for insightful discussions on human rights and for reading an earlier draft.

Special thanks to Thomas and James for always asking how the book was going and telling me I could do it and to my amazing husband for reading every draft of every chapter no matter what else was going on.

FOREWORD

The criminal justice system has always struggled to understand the needs of victims. Part of the problem lies in the use of language. "What's in a name?", asks Emma Forbes in her Introduction. Quite a lot is the simple answer to her question. The word "victim" is not a suitable term within a court of law, as she points out. The court has to be guided throughout by the presumption of innocence. The prosecutor has to respect that principle too, as do the police. This means that a person cannot be referred to there as a victim unless and until that presumption has been overcome. That is why we use the terms "complainant" and "complainer" instead. But the fact is that those who are brave enough to complain to the police and to come to court in that capacity are almost always victims too.

I was acutely aware, when taking evidence from a complainer in gender violence cases during my time as an Advocate Depute in the High Court of Justiciary that I was not there to represent the complainer, however compelling her case might seem to me to be. I did my best, by careful and patient questioning and by maintaining eye contact with her throughout the whole process as we went over in public all the most intimate details, to set her at ease. But this was done at a distance across the court room, not by standing beside her or offering her any other kind of support. I had to leave it to others to look after her before and after her appearance in court. For those others she was still seen as a complainer until the verdict was announced. I could not speak to her during any adjournments, and I had to remain detached from her even at the end of the trial. I did not think that gender had much to do with this. It was the system I had to work with, and it was the system that left her friendless and alone.

Decades have passed since those days, and much has been done by means of legislation and policy changes to remove the glass barriers and to redress the balance in favour of the most vulnerable. This is especially with regard to gender violence and domestic abuse, in particular. But there are still problems that have not gone away and, as this perceptive and carefully researched book shows, much still remains to be done. Its value lies in the fact that the writer's understanding has been gathered at first hand from her experience in practice as a prosecutor. So her research has been based on her observations of what actually happens before, in and after court. This provided her with the ideal setting for her discussion with victims at each stage in the process. She knew and understood what they were talking about because she was there too. The result is a vivid and compelling account of the emotions which pull in so many directions as each case evolves, and of the tensions that are created by the time it takes to resolve it.

Against that background the writer seeks to address what she sees as a stubborn misalignment between the policy vision, the legal framework and women's reality. So there are recommendations. They range from small practical changes to improvements in education and reforms to law and to policy. For this reason alone the book deserves to be widely read. But there is much more to it than that. The way it is written draws the reader into the subject in a way that a mere textbook cannot do. Here is someone who feels deeply about the way women are still failed by the system, and who seeks to encourage others to think as deeply about how to address these failures as she does. The way forward, in other words, lies in the hearts and minds of those who practice in this field. I hope that in that way the book will achieve the success that it so obviously deserves.

David Hope
September 2021

INTRODUCTION

The first time I visited Glasgow Sheriff Court, uncomfortable in ill-fitting black clothes, my feet pinched in cheap heels, I sat in the public gallery of the custody court and prepared for great excitement. As a keen law student, I was enthusiastic about the opportunity to shadow a solicitor in one of the busiest courts in Europe. In fact, it was bewildering and boring. The custody court is a cavernous room in the basement, and the public gallery is set back from the body of the court. Sitting in the second row, I could not hear anything. I watched for hours as a troop of lawyers came forward, mumbled, and retreated like dejected theatre actors at an audition. Not only was it dull, it was frustrating because I did not understand what was happening.

Fast forward two years, I was often the newly qualified prosecutor in the same courtroom. My experience was very different. Within the well of the court, there is a buzz, camaraderie, focus, and spiky, engaging debate. It is a privilege to prosecute in the public interest. Whilst there is often banter with solicitors on both sides of the table, there is a deep sentiment of duty instilled in prosecutors and those representing the accused. All of this is lost on the public. Perceptions of court come from (American) television dramas and bear little resemblance to reality. Members of the public, complainers giving evidence, and accused are all involved in the court process and yet still leave the building unclear on the process. What just happened? Unlike television, there is no helpful recap. Support agencies like Victim Support and Witness Service work hard to help those attending court demystify the process. However, for victims of domestic abuse, the barriers to understanding the process are compounded by the impact that court decisions have on their home life and the lives of their children and the compelling effect this has on their emotional response to court.

I became the first full-time prosecutor within the Domestic Abuse Pilot Court in Glasgow in 2004. My understanding of domestic abuse was so scant that I thought I did not know anyone who had been affected. My strategy was to deal with one case at a time and treat each person coming to court as an individual. I started at the beginning. I read Erin Pizzey, Ellen Pence, and the Dobashes and attended my first Scottish Women's Aid (SWA) conference. I tried to learn from victims and their supporters. This made me sensitive to the public/private nexus in these cases, and the most difficult consideration is often deciding where the public interest[1] lies in such a victim-led approach.

It also made me think about why it is so hard to achieve good outcomes despite legislative and policy advances. Police reports relating to physical assaults and threatening and abusive behaviour contain intensely private details of family life: a window into someone else's inner sanctum. Such feelings are intensified as reports detail long-term emotional and psychological abuse (Ontiveros, 1995). Victims may be asked to share personal details of sleeping arrangements, daily routines, and private messages, comprising: 'an individualised package of behaviours ... by the person who knows her most intimately' (Tolmie, 2017, p. 7). This is uncomfortable (Hoyle, 2000). It is a challenge for the police officer and the prosecutor that becomes magnified for those in the courtroom when faced with the raw, unedited reality of women and children's emotional response to abuse. Despite best efforts and increased training, the discomfort of professionals polarises victims and leads to profound feelings of being unheard and disbelieved. Recognising and dealing with emotion appears to me to be the nub of what is missing from the justice response.

PURPOSE OF THIS BOOK

This book tells the story of the justice response from the perspective of a victim of domestic abuse: from the initial call to the police, waiting for court, procedural hearings, the trial, and until the ultimate outcome. It is a progressive area in which there have been developments in social and political understanding of the state's remit in private life following intimate abuse. In telling the victims' story, it is important to understand the legal and policy landscape. The apparent sweep of progress on the public stage is juxtaposed with the private struggle of individuals who continue to face barriers to justice. Drawing on in-depth interviews with women who have experienced domestic abuse and those who support them, this book identifies enduring challenges and makes practical recommendations.

Chapters One and Two provide the context for women's stories. Based on a 40-year timeline of the UK response to domestic abuse, these chapters set the scene of the policy, legal, social, and academic responses to victims of gender violence, in general, and domestic abuse, in particular. Chapters Three–Five tell women's stories of the impact of reporting to the police, going to court, and the aftermath. Chapter Three considers the risks and safety implications for women of reporting to the police and the fault lines in current communication with victims as they wait *for* court. Chapter Four narrates stories of women waiting *at* court and how such waiting influences their ability to give evidence and reflects how they are perceived. Chapter Five discusses different potential outcomes, from an early decision not to proceed to a late negotiated plea or a trial and sentence. Chapter Six argues that legislative change has limited potential until structural inequalities are addressed and the best hope for victims lies in a more emotionally intuitive response through consistently delivered procedural justice. It considers potential developments, including problem-solving courts and closer alignment of the civil and criminal courts. Chapter Seven concludes with the impact of informed debate on gender inequality within criminal justice and identifies how we can move beyond 'glass walls'.

WHY GLASSWALLS?

The gendered and under-recognised nature of barriers faced by women is similar to the 'glass ceiling' which second-wave feminism highlighted 40 years ago (Fielding, 2018) as a seemingly invisible, structural barrier to women progressing equally in the workplace. Domestic abuse is both publicly recognised and privately ongoing and imperceptible. At once, women are offered support and encouraged to report and, at the same time, they report 'feeling crazy' because ongoing abusive behaviour is not acknowledged. I describe this as living behind glass walls.

Glass Walls is both the ideological framework explored throughout this book and the name of a collaborative community art project with victims of domestic abuse. The premise of this book is that the barriers faced by women in the court process are gendered and structural. Their stories unfold through the images between each chapter. These images were developed to engage a wider audience through a creative medium and became part of a colourful stained-glass exhibition.[2]

Glass Walls, the project, is a collaboration with the Daisy Project, a grassroots support project for victims of domestic abuse, and WASPS art studio. Professional stained-glass artists provided weekly art classes at Daisy and the women each created their own piece. A collage of their work formed part of the final exhibition, alongside a triptych of stained-glass panels set in light boxes. The large panels are an artistic depiction of societal responses to domestic abuse from the 1970s to the present. The exhibition was created through grant funding and charitable donations and has been gifted to Glasgow Museums. Proceeds of this book will help rehabilitative art classes at Daisy to continue.

WHAT IS DOMESTIC ABUSE?

This book adopts a gendered and legal understanding of domestic abuse.[3] Social and legal responses can be distinct, without being contradictory.

In England and Wales, there was a shift in 2013 from 'domestic violence' to 'domestic violence and abuse' (Home Office, 2013). The definition of domestic abuse goes beyond the physical to recognise psychological, sexual, financial, and emotional abuse within intimate partner relationships (irrespective of gender or sexuality). The Domestic Abuse Act 2021 extends this definition to include ex-partners. The Crown Prosecution Service (CPS) adopts a Violence Against Women and Girls (VAWG) Strategy, based on the UN Convention,[4] to inform their investigation and prosecution of domestic abuse as an example of offending that: 'has been identified as being committed primarily but not exclusively by men against women' (HM Government, 2016).

Similarly, the Scottish government recognises domestic abuse as a gendered problem (*Equally Safe*, 2018). The current Joint Protocol (2017) between Police Scotland and Crown Office and Procurator Fiscal Service (COPFS) contains a definition of domestic abuse which includes physical, verbal, sexual, psychological, and financial abuse. It applies to (ex)partners, men and women. It does not distinguish between same-sex and heterosexual relationships, but it recognises a specific dynamic of intimate partner abuse and does not include familial abuse within its definition.

Both jurisdictions have shown that it is possible for the law to remain gender-neutral whilst adopting a gendered policy understanding of the realities of predominant victimisation. Although, some commentators consider this falls short (Bishop, 2016b). This is explored further in Chapter One.

WHAT'S IN A NAME?

The court process in England and Wales refers to complainants; in Scotland, complainers. This book adopts the term 'victim'. Feminist literature on domestic abuse is divided on appropriate terminology. Some refer to 'victims' and many prefer 'victim-survivor' (for a discussion, see Gondolf & Fisher, 1988; Burton, 2008).[5] Personally, the annual domestic homicide statistics make me uncomfortable referring to victims as 'survivors'; like 'battling' an illness, it is not always possible to control the outcome. These are social terms and as I have engaged directly with those who have experienced abuse to conduct this research, I judged it sensitive and apposite to refer to victims in my discussion. However, as Lord Hope rightly oberves, this is not a suitable term this is not a suitable term within a court of law, where the presumption of innocence is a basic tenet of our justice system and the rules of evidence are clear. There are increasing references to victims' rights in the formal process but broadly in relation to legislation providing *service* rights within the process; it has not affected court vocabulary. Throughout this book, reference to legal texts or the court process may refer to complainants/ers, but I have broadly adopted social meanings.

WHAT DOES IT MEAN TO HAVE AGENCY?

Defining women's agency is problematic in relation to violence against women as views are divided about whether women ought to be cast as victims or assertive agents (Schneider, 2000). Hoyle and Sanders (2000) advocate a model of victim empowerment which is centred on individual choice and does not prefer the public interest (see also Mills, 1998). There have also been warnings that a social mentality of victimisation could emerge in which all women are perceived victims (Mythen, 2011; Stanko, 2000).

There is scope for victims to retain greater agency *within the court process*,[6] without compromising the public interest, the rights of the accused, or the independence of the court. I suggest that there are three aspects to agency for victims within the court process. A definition ought to include, first, the capacity for informed choice; second, freedom from further criminal conduct; and, third, a means to be heard. Informed choice means that when a woman makes a call to the police to report domestic abuse or is asked by the police to provide a statement, she knows the consequences of her action: that the criminal justice response is predictable, understandable, and transparent. Freedom from further criminal conduct means that the act of reporting an allegation of criminal conduct ought to stop further abuse. The interview data in this book suggest that far from bringing domestic abuse into the open, reporting criminality represents an opportunity for the accused to coercively control his victim through abuse of the system. Agency within the court process encompasses having your voice heard. This may be within the formal setting of a trial but need not be. Ways in which this can be achieved are explored throughout this book.

THE NATURE AND SCALE OF DOMESTIC ABUSE

The nature and impact of domestic abuse are increasingly understood and a government report estimated that the overall social and economic 'cost' in England and Wales in one year (2017) was £66 billion (Oliver, Alexander, Roe, & Wlasny, 2019). Across the UK, governments recognise domestic abuse as an endemic problem (HM Government, 2016; Scottish Government, 2016). Increased reports of domestic abuse as a direct result of the Covid-19 lockdown and confinement with abusers have led the Executive Director of United Nations Women to describe gender-based violence as the 'shadow pandemic' (Mlambo-Ngcuka, 2020). Nevertheless, understanding the scale of the problem is difficult because of the hidden, suppressed nature of the offending. Governments rely on reported cases, which we know represent a small proportion of the overall number, as under-reporting remains chronic. Moreover, differing definitions mean that even within the UK, governments are not counting the same offending.

Police Scotland responds to a domestic abuse call every nine minutes.[7] In England and Wales, the police recorded 1,288,018 domestic abuse-related incidents between March 2019 and March 2020. In total, 59% were reported crimes. It is estimated that 4% of adults in England and Wales experience abuse by an (ex)partner.[8] In 2019, 80 women were killed by an (ex) partner,[9] and in 2021, Jess Phillips, MP, highlighted the scale of men's violence against women when she read out the names of 118 women killed in 2020 by a man.[10]

There have been some attempts to 'count' (Stanko, 2001; Walby & Myhill, 2000; Walby, Towers, & Francis, 2016), but methods remain limited (Hoyle, 2011, 2012). For example, SWA has conducted a survey of its service provision on one day each year since 2009. The annual census does not give an indication of the scale of domestic abuse in Scotland, but it provides a snapshot of those in refuge, those being supported in the community, and those turned away from refuge due to lack of resources.

The introduction of national crime surveys has been attributed to developing knowledge of victims and particularly women's experiences of victimisation (Walklate, 2011; Zedner, 2002). Following the pilot victimisation study in 1977, the first British Crime Survey was conducted in 1982. The first Scottish Crime and Justice Survey followed in 1983. It is a crude way of gathering data as it relies on individuals' perceptions of their experiences and their willingness to report victim experiences. Earlier studies tended to focus on crimes, and honest responses may be affected by whether there are others present when the survey questions are asked (Walby & Myhill, 2000). There is also arguably still a social stigma.

The crime survey has been criticised for contributing to a 'Victims R Us' mentality (Mythen, 2011; Stanko, 2000) and failing to capture the 'impact' of victimisation (Hoyle, 2012; Zedner, 2002). That said, it provides key data on societal attitudes to crime (Zedner, 2002). The crime survey is a solid indicator of the scale of the problem – beyond reported cases – and should help individuals to recognise aspects of abuse they may not have acknowledged, including psychological and financial abuse.

METHODOLOGY

The foundation of this book is doctoral research conducted at the University of Glasgow within the College of Social and Political Sciences. The research adopted a mixed-method approach that triangulated:

- in-depth qualitative interviews with victims of domestic abuse and their support workers (n = 34: 19 workers and 15 victims);

- a socio-legal narrative of government, policy, and social responses; and

- auto-ethnographic practitioner experience.

By interviewing both victims of abuse and their support workers, I aimed to ensure a safe ethical position,[11] where participants had access to therapeutic support. In fact, I unravelled a mesh of identities, as the importance of (in)formal support networks became clear. Women's Aid's ethos of 'Women-Helping-Women-Helping-Women' (SWA, 2017) is strong across the voluntary sector in this area, and many of the support and advocacy workers I interviewed disclosed experience of abuse. Missing from the data set is the voice of women who do not report and those who report but do not accept support. The women have been anonymised; all the names in this book are pseudonyms.

A socio-legal narrative of the wider response to domestic abuse provides context for the women's stories and shows the disconnect between the apparent pace of progress and enduring barriers for victims who report.[12] It illustrates the pace and direction of progress and provides an analytical framework for discussion of the data findings.

Much is made of the need for a holistic approach to justice, particularly in cases of domestic abuse. Nevertheless, divisions are rife: England and Scotland, criminal law and civil law, victims' rights and accused's rights (broadly victimology and penology), academia and practice, and third-sector and formal justice agencies. It is perhaps a little overwhelming to try to reconcile them, and there is a risk of confusion. My focus is on the victim's journey through the criminal justice process. Interviews were carried out in Scotland, but a number of influences have led me to consider the merits of a cross-referenced, bigger picture. Dual-qualified in English and Scots law and a prosecutor with an academic itch, knowledge of the process comes from practice rather than books. If an assertion is made without reference to an academic text or the empirical data, it is probably the anecdotal observation of a prosecutor.

DEFINING FEMINISM – IT'S PERSONAL

On her appointment as UN ambassador in 2014, Emma Watson defined feminism as: 'The belief that men and women should have equal rights and opportunities. It is the theory of the political, economic and social equality of the sexes'.[13]

Debates on the relationship between gender and sex, intersectionality, and the development of feminist ideologies are beyond the scope of this text. This book adopts a simple assumption that gender equality is a fundamental human right. It recognises that treating everyone the same does not always lead to equality and that domestic abuse is a gendered problem. We know that women are more likely than men to be victims of domestic abuse and treating both the same evades equality.

In her foreword for the Scottish Feminist Judgements, Lady Carmichael is open about the challenges of being a female decision-maker within a historically male-dominated environment and the benefits of not being the most feminist person in the room (Cowan, Kennedy, & Munro, 2019). We need both radical and moderate feminists. The glass ceiling within the legal profession would be lower without the quiet determination of judges like Lady Carmichael who inspire a younger female cohort by working through the system and making the path seem manageable. It is in complementary approaches that we progress. I hope that if any of the feminist academics who have inspired me are reading this, they can forgive my shortcomings and recognise that I work 'within' the establishment. I believe that domestic abuse is predominantly and more profoundly experienced by women and children and that it is a gendered blight on our society.

This book has been written as two stories: the story of the coherent, but sometimes misplaced, reform of law and policy, and the story of the barriers women face when they report domestic abuse as a crime. First-person accounts of reporting domestic abuse throughout this book give an insight into the impact of reporting and the ongoing trauma that it provokes. This is not my story to tell, and I hope that by using the words of women with lived experience and the beautiful illustrations they inspired, I have remained true to them.

NOTES

1. England and Wales: Code for Crown Prosecutors contains a public interest test (Crown Prosecution Service, 2013). Available at: The Code for Crown Prosecutors|The Crown Prosecution Service (cps.gov.uk). Scotland, the Prosecution Code (Crown Office, 2018) contains a public interest test. Available at: Microsoft Word – Prosecution Code _Final 180412_.doc (copfs.gov.uk).

2. Available at: www.glasswallsart.com.

3. For a general overview of the literature on domestic violence/abuse, see Gadd, 2017.

4. Convention on the Elimination of Discrimination Against Women (CEDAW), UN, 1979, see Chapter One.

5. Much of the literature will refer to accused as perpetrators. I have referred to accused pre-trial and perpetrators or offenders for convicted persons.

6. For a wider discussion on women's agency within an abusive relationship, see Westmarland (2015).

7. The average number of incidents reported to Police Scotland annually is between 58,000 and 61,000. In 2018–2019, 60,641 incidents were recorded; an increase of 2% on the previous year.

8. Statistics drawn from reported police figures and the British Crime Survey and available from the Office for National Statistics (ONS). Available at: www.ons.gov.uk.

9. Available from the ONS: www.ons.gov.uk.

10. Part of a debate for International Women's Day, 2021 – reported at Jess Phillips: Society has 'just accepted' dead women – BBC News. This figure includes all male violence against women and is not limited to domestic abuse.

11. There is further information on my ethical position within the resource page of www.glasswallsart.com, or the thesis can be download from the British Library (www.ethos.bl.uk).

12. To access an interactive timeline of legal, social, policy, academic, and international responses to domestic abuse over a 40-year period, visit www.glasswallsart.com.

13. See www.unwomen.org, available at: Emma Watson Gender equality is your issue too|UN Women – Headquarters.

Chapter One

THE POLICY APPROACH

INTRODUCTION

Police officers in the 1970s routinely dealt with men accused of hitting their wives by driving them to the edge of town, emptying their pockets and leaving them to walk home. The rationale was that the man would have cooled down and sobered up by the time he got back and domestic abuse was not seen as a criminal matter (Burton, 2016). Pizzey (1974, p. 116) detected 'a wide gap between what the law says and what the police will actually do'. It was, after all, 'just a domestic'.[1] Victims of domestic abuse have, until relatively recently, endured compound denial of their status. Not only was domestic abuse 'the violence of privacy' within society (Schneider, 2000, p. 87), but victims were 'forgotten players' (Walklate, 2011) within the court process, treated similarly to members of the public or used as tools for the prosecution (Garland, 2001; Rock, 2011; Shapland, 1986). There has been a significant shift from this description of 1970s policing to the current picture. Today, UK government policies recognise domestic abuse as an aspect of gendered violence against women and third-sector support agencies receive government funding. The police response has revolutionised: specially trained officers conduct risk assessments, prioritise victim safety at multi-agency conferences, refer victims to support agencies and victim advocates, and report criminal offences to specially accredited domestic abuse prosecutors (Burman, 2018). Nevertheless, there remains a stubborn gap between ambitions to improve the justice response and women's lived reality of the process.

The purpose of this chapter (together with the legal backdrop in Chapter Two) is to set the scene for the women's stories that follow. It summarises policy changes in tackling domestic abuse in particular and vulnerable victims more generally. It contextualises political aims and the impact of feminism thus far. Sociological and philosophical perspectives have framed the current understanding of domestic abuse as a continuum of 'coercive control' (Stark, 2007) and predominantly gendered offending (Hester, 2013).

By the end of this chapter, you should understand:

- An historic perspective of the early campaign and its impact.
- Key developments in the victims' rights movement.
- The core policies that inform the criminal justice approach to domestic abuse (multi-agency working, specialist courts, victim advocates, training, the development of risk indicators).
- Current government policy in Scotland and England and Wales on domestic abuse.

This chapter is divided into four parts: the first part charts the influence of the feminist campaign in the 1970s and how it set the scene for recognition of domestic abuse as a public wrong. The second covers the development of specific victim policies and recognition of victims' rights. The third part describes the growth of a multi-agency response and how that influenced the introduction of specialist courts, victim advocates, training, and safety planning. Finally, the fourth part situates the current gendered policies and training framework.

I: EARLY YEARS: CONSCIOUSNESS-RAISING FROM THE GRASSROOTS

The first women's refuge in the UK was opened by Erin Pizzey in Chiswick, London, in 1971. Pizzey was a feminist activist whose memoir of the early years, *Scream Quietly or the Neighbours Will Hear*, was published in 1974. It was a short, unassuming paperback published by Penguin for general circulation. It was read by housewives and commuters. It shocked. It raised awareness in a new and high-impact way. It remains the seminal feminist text providing narratives of women's experience of domestic abuse at a time when it remained largely hidden. It inspired women across the country and was a key influence on the opening of refuges. Chiswick refuge was the precursor in England and Wales to the charity Refuge that still supports women and children seeking shelter from abuse. In England and Wales, the provision of refuge has remained distinct from the campaigning arm of the Women's Aid Federation for England (WAFE). In Scotland, refuge is provided by Women's Aid groups under the umbrella of SWA.

In 1973, two members of the Glasgow Women's Liberation group (part of the Women's Liberation Movement – the genesis for Women's Aid groups in Scotland) visited Chiswick Women's Refuge:

> *We drove home to Glasgow, I remember. Actually, we were both weeping from the sort of things she told us and this realisation that we had that there really was a big problem here and that nobody was doing anything about it.*[2]

By December, they had founded their own refuge in Edinburgh – the first in Scotland – and one opened in Glasgow in early 1974. That there was a growing need to 'do something' was unsurprising.

Indeed, the 1970s was a decade of practical steps and consciousness-raising – of forging collective goals – in which women recognised inequalities and identified common ground (Renzetti, 2013). The organisation of the first *Reclaim the Night* march,[3] a defiant stance against the lack of police progress in the notorious Yorkshire Ripper case, symbolises the shift. As a period of reflection and foundation-building, it was useful (Browne, 2016) but is distinct from later periods of awareness-raising to a wider audience. It is interesting that funding was made available to refuges in the late 1970s – when there was political unrest, a build up to strike action (Marr, 2008) and the beginnings of crime control governance (Simon, 2007).

Following the general election in 1979 and a change to a Conservative government, funding was not prioritised and the 1980s saw a relative lack of progress for victims' movements (Rock, 2004): the victim remained almost invisible in the court process (Shapland, 1986). Nevertheless, the 1980s was a period of consolidation and mobilisation for grassroots organisations (Breitenbach & Mackay, 2001). For example, Victim Support was established as the first national support body for victims of crime. Their new National Code of Practice set a basic standard for victim care, and their first conference in 1981 drove a UK-wide approach and called the government to account. In 1987, the Home Office initiated core funding that aligned support to victims of crime with government policy and protected Victim Support as a charitable organisation. Their key funding stream is now the Police and Crime Commissioners, and they remain reliant on charitable donations.

As early as 1979, the root causes of domestic abuse were being situated in broader cultural and societal challenges to gender inequality and patriarchal hierarchies (Dobash & Dobash, 1979), and emotional and psychological abuse was highlighted. In 1988, Kelly described violence against women as an 'epidemic'. Given what we now know about violence against women and girls worldwide (Mlambo-Ngcuka, 2020), it could sadly be described as a pandemic. The relevance of Kelly's research today is both impressive and disheartening, illustrating wisdom at a time when violence against women was barely acknowledged, yet also highlighting the slow progress since. As domestic abuse was gaining recognition as a societal problem, wider scholarship was becoming increasingly gender aware.

II: A DEVELOPING CONCEPT OF VICTIMS' RIGHTS

Policies in both England and Wales and Scotland have been influenced by international and European Union (EU) principles. The United Nations Declaration of Basic Principles of Justice for Victims of Crime and Abuse of Power in November 1985 provided a global definition of 'victim' and called for compassion, respect, and dignity for victims of crime, whether or not a perpetrator is apprehended and brought to justice.[4]

The principles of the 1985 convention were not initially embedded and victims remained a tool for the prosecution (Shapland, 1986). Commentators blamed the Thatcher government for victims being framed as ancillary to the criminal justice process: a robust approach to crime assumed that preventing crime helped minimise victimisation, but there was no specific focus on victim policies (Rock, 2004).

By the 1990s, the police began to adopt a specialist response by identifying Domestic Violence Liaison Officers and issuing guidance to officers, but the police response was focussed on incidents of violence. Nevertheless, the Victim Charter for England and Wales in 1990, introduced by the new Major Conservative administration, was a significant shift. It was the first attempt to bring together all elements of the criminal justice response and declared a statement of rights for how victims should be treated, although it did not have a legal basis (Fenwick, 1997). The revised Victim Charter for England and Wales (1996) has been attributed to John Major's personal commitment to a more rights-based approach for victims of crime (Rock, 2004) and explicitly linked victims' rights to a statement of service standards. Service rights can broadly be understood as procedural rights within the court process (a right to information and a right to be treated fairly) rather than a right of participation, which would suggest victims play a more active role in the process (I. Edwards, 2004). An example of a right of participation would be a right to legal representation (Raitt, 2010, 2013) or a right to have views heard. Both are distinct from the promotion of victims' welfare outside of court (Elias, 1986). Increasingly, Victim Support was recognising the importance of securing service rights for victims going to court (Fenwick, 1997).

New grassroots organisations also emerged. In London, *Justice for Women* was founded in 1990 as a campaigning organisation to support women who kill their (ex)partners (Itzin, 2000; Westmarland, 2015).[5] In Scotland, *Engender* was founded in 1993 as a feminist policy and advocacy organisation to promote gender equality.[6]

Alongside these small, feminist charities, at the international level, the UN Declaration on Violence Against Women in 1993 contributed to understanding gender violence as 'a cause and consequence of gender inequality' (Westmarland, 2015) and informed the Scottish definition of domestic abuse. The UK commitment to the Beijing Platform for Action in

1995, to promote women's human rights, has also influenced the pace of policy development in England and Wales and Scotland (Matczak, Hatzidimitriadou, & Lindsay, 2011).

Membership of the EU conferred legal obligations, including implementation of EU Directives and adoption of EU jurisprudence, but did not make a great impact on UK jurisprudence around victims until the Human Rights Act 1998 was passed into law under the first Blair New Labour administration: a wholesale incorporation of the rights set down in the European Convention on Human Rights (ECHR) into domestic law. The convention includes a right not to be subject to torture or inhuman and degrading treatment[7] but also preserves an individual's right to respect for privacy in their own home.[8] The impact of the UK withdrawal from the EU (Brexit) on victim policies is a textbook in itself, and it is too early to predict the extent of the fall-out. Organisations such as the Equality and Human Rights Commission[9] are concerned that the loss of the *Charter of Fundamental Human Rights of the European Union* (European Parliament, 2000) will compromise the development of human rights, as jurisprudence from the Court of Justice of the EU will no longer be enforceable (Coppel, 2018). Nevertheless, the fact that the ECHR was enshrined in UK law by the Human Rights Act 1998 means that basic rights are protected.

The New Labour manifesto (1997) committed to a referendum on devolved powers for Scotland and Wales. Scottish devolution in 1999 was structurally important in strengthening the autonomy of the legislative process (Charles & Mackay, 2013), increased legislation and criminalisation (Chalmers & Leverick, 2013; Chalmers, 2014) and influenced the pace of change in relation to victim policy, in general, and domestic abuse policy, in particular. It has been attributed to, 'more participatory political and institutional formations' (Burman & Johnstone, 2015). Domestic abuse was debated during Holyrood's first parliamentary session (Mackay, 2010), and a National Strategy to Address Domestic Abuse in Scotland was published to coincide with the new parliament (Mackay, 2010), having been commissioned by the Scottish Office in 1998 (Greenan, 2004).

By the turn of the century, there was a promising trend that recognised some procedural rights for victims in the court process and increased awareness of the need to train police officers in the dynamics of domestic violence/abuse. Both Westminster and Holyrood had policies on domestic violence/abuse (Greenan, 2004; Home Office, 1999; Matczak et al., 2011; Scottish Executive, 2000; Strickland, 2012). Third-sector agencies remained on the fringe of the formal court response, but the police appetite to learn set the scene for multi-agency working and a more coordinated response.

III: A MULTI-AGENCY APPROACH AND THE RISK MODEL

The combined impact of devolution and a New Labour government with a large parliamentary majority influenced feelings of cautious optimism as the millennium dawned. The Scottish Parliament sought to recognise domestic abuse 'as part of an overall strategy' to tackle violence against women (Scottish Executive, 2000, 2003). Funding was contingent on the local government working in partnership (Greenan, 2004) which influenced the strong multi-agency approach that developed (Brooks-Hay, 2018; Lombard & Macmillan, 2013; Robinson, 2006a). Similarly, the communitarian approach (Shepard & Pence, 1999) fostered by New Labour in Westminster encouraged regional responses, and welfare politics thrived (Lavalette & Mooney, 1999) in an environment that promoted multi-agency working.

Thus, conditions in both jurisdictions were amenable to the Duluth model of a coordinated community response to domestic abuse (Pence & McDonnell, 2000; Shepard & Pence, 1999) that emerged from the United States. Developed by Ellen Pence in Duluth, Minnesota, in 1981, the model was labelled a 'batterer intervention program' in line with American terminology. With a feminist underpinning, the premise was simple: a multidisciplinary approach to tackling domestic abuse predicated on the recognition that violence against women and children is gendered. Pence developed the 'power and control' wheel that remains widely adopted by advocates and practitioners to explain abusive behaviours, reflecting the growing recognition that domestic abuse needs a holistic response. Lack of a joint philosophy is a potential barrier to effective coordination and can breed tensions (Shepard & Pence, 1999). This explains some of the discomfort associated with activist workers, through stakeholder engagement, aligning with 'insider' (Cuthbert & Irving, 2001, p. 58) criminal justice agencies (Bumiller, 2008). Nevertheless, grassroots agencies supporting women who have experienced domestic abuse have evolved as 'critical friends' to formal justice agencies and increasingly contribute to policy and law reform.

Specialist Courts

The adoption of more coordinated responses paved the way for specialist domestic abuse courts, which in turn strengthened multi-agency relationships (Robinson, 2006a). Specialist courts provide training to judges, clerks, prosecutors, and solicitors; encourage agencies to work more closely together to ensure victim safety and facilitate engagement through information-sharing; and, in the event of conviction, make perpetrators more accountable through tailored sentencing (Connelly, 2008; 2011). The aim is to remove cases from an overburdened 'conveyer-belt' court (Packer, 1964) and provide a more tailored and thoughtful response. Five specialist domestic violence courts in England and Wales adopted three different models – fast-tracking, clustering, and tailored specialist courts – depending on the size and caseload of the jurisdiction (Cook, Burton, Robinson, & Vallely, 2004). The first 'cluster court' was in Leeds in 1999, followed by Cardiff, Derby, Wolverhampton, and Croyden, West London. Their success influenced the introduction of the first Scottish court in Glasgow in 2004 (Robinson, 2006a). Support for specialist domestic abuse courts is not unanimous[10] although evaluation was broadly positive (Cook et al., 2004; Reid Howie, 2007) and the opportunity for a national model has been missed.[11] Budgetary constraints and the austerity agenda following the 2008 financial crash have impacted on all aspects of criminal justice, including the specialist court (BBC News, 2010; Bettinson, 2016a).

Despite the lack of a consistent roll-out programme for specialist courts, new problem-solving court initiatives continue to emerge in pilot format, and the Westminster government's White Paper on the Police, Crime, Sentencing and Courts Bill 2021 commits to five new problem-solving courts to tackle drug misuse, domestic abuse, and the needs of vulnerable female offenders (Ministry of Justice, 2020). In Scotland, there are drug and alcohol problem-solving courts (Centre for Jusitcie Innovation, 2017), but the specialist domestic abuse courts do not adopt the problem-solving court model. The potential of integrated, multi-agency family justice centres has been explored (Hoyle & Palmer, 2014), and the opening of the unique justice centre in Inverness in 2020 offers an opportunity to learn from a more holistic approach with many key agencies collocated in one building.[12]

The difference between a problem-solving court and a specialist approach is the monitoring of community-based sentences. In a problem-solving court, judges are 'at the centre of rehabilitation' (Centre for Justice Innovation, 2015). Their focus is on procedural fairness to the accused and a structured, supervised – in court – rehabilitation programme. Despite positive evaluation (Centre for Justice Innovation, 2016) and an aim to make sentencing more accountable, the courts have been described as 'not one thing' and more of a 'diverse family of court models' (Centre for Justice Innovation, 2020) although they usually rely on multi-agency input and are outcome focussed (Centre for Justice Innovation, 2020). Problem-solving courts are usually built on a specialist court model (Eunson, Murray, Malloch, McIvor, & Graham, 2018). An increase in problem-solving courts may offer greater hope of a more specialist approach to domestic abuse[13] which is arguably the foundation for future reform, as we will see in Chapter Six.

Victim Advocates

A key component of the specialist response has been the development of victim advocates, introduced to complement the specialist courts. Independent Domestic Violence Advocates (IDVAs) in England and Wales and Independent Domestic Abuse Advocates (IDAAs) in Scotland provide specialist independent support and have a dual function: individual advocacy to help victims through the court process and institutional advocacy, to improve policy and practice in relation to the court response to domestic abuse. The main purpose of IDVAs/IDAAs is:

> *to address the safety of victims at high risk of harm … to secure their safety and the safety of their children. Serving as a victim's primary point of contact, IDVAs normally work with their clients from the point of crisis to assess the level of risk, discuss the range of suitable options and develop*

> *safety plans. They are pro-active in implementing the plans, which address immediate safety, including practical steps to protect themselves and their children, as well as longer-term solutions.*
> *(SafeLives, national definition)*

Victim advocates and grassroots support workers are distinct in the focus of their support, noting that an individual may fulfil both roles. Both are proponents of a person-centred ethos, where individual needs inform a nuanced approach. However, whilst grassroots workers support women with a range of practical and emotional needs, the advocacy model focuses on support through the criminal justice process and has been piloted for victims of domestic abuse (Hester & Westmarland, 2005) and sexual assault (Brooks & Burman, 2017). Advocacy denotes different meaning across jurisdictions (Brooks & Burman, 2017). Whilst there may be no precise definition of 'advocacy', it borrows language and meaning from the courtroom, in terms of being a voice for victims. It usually contains key components: independence, proactive outreach, safety planning, information provision, risk assessment, crisis intervention, a coordinated community response, and institutional advocacy (Robinson & Payton, 2016; Scottish Government, 2017b, include training and knowledge of local resources).

The role of the advocate has developed and expanded across organisations, beyond supporting specialist courts, with the introduction of a formal training programme in victim advocacy, since *SafeLives* was founded in 2005[14]:

> *The big idea was to start from risk. If you understand the level of risk that victims face, those at high risk of serious harm or murder can get the fastest help. This was different to most domestic abuse services at the time.*

SafeLives pioneered the first risk indicator checklist (RIC) which has increased the prominence of the risk assessment as a means of assessing safety needs and has professionalised the role of IDVAs/IDAAs. Levels of advocacy support across the UK are inconsistent and *SafeLives* reports that only four police forces across England and Wales have enough IDVAs to support all high-risk victims.

Training

SafeLives has also become responsible for training on domestic abuse to criminal justice professionals and accredits specialist advocacy workers, to provide court support to victims of domestic abuse. They have worked with the College of Policing in England and Wales and Police Scotland to create a training course specifically for police officers – *Domestic Abuse Matters*. Crucially, the training aims to be: 'a cultural change programme designed to create long term, sustainable improvements and consistency in the response to domestic abuse'(*SafeLives*). It covers risk assessment, victim-blaming, minimisation, and how to recognise signs of coercive control. Whilst the course has received positive feedback from police officers, access to the course remains uneven. COPFS has worked with *SafeLives* to develop a bespoke accredited training course for prosecutors in Scotland. The course is in-depth and includes spending time with an advocacy service. In both jurisdictions, there is reciprocal learning between IDVAs/IDAAs and police/prosecutors.[15] Following the publication of the 2020 inspectorate report on obtaining evidence in domestic abuse cases (HMCPSI & HMICFRS, 2020), *SafeLives* called on the government to fund *Domestic Abuse Matters* training for *all* police officers and prosecutors.

Across the UK, judicial training remains judge led and closed to scrutiny. Thus, the extent of judicial training on the dynamic of domestic abuse is unknown. Both law societies offer training on domestic abuse, but it is not mandatory, and solicitors can appear in the criminal and civil courts with no specialist training. Across all aspects of the justice process, whilst some training initiatives are encouraging, the lack of mandatory training means provision is inconsistent.

Multi-agency Conferences and Risk Assessments

The RIC was pioneered by *SafeLives* and was based on the analysis of domestic homicides to predict risk factors for domestic abuse. Initially known as the CAADA Dash Risk Checklist,[16] it asks 24 questions designed to elicit information relating to key risk factors affecting women's safety and the likelihood of re-victimisation, including the presence of children, use of a weapon, previous 'incidents', sexual violence, and cruelty to pets. It is complemented by an abuse severity grid that provides a framework to help IDAA/IDVAs to identify high-risk factors (*SafeLives*).

The risk checklist was modified to become the Victim Risk Indicator Form in 2002 (Robinson, 2006b), whereby police officers started to ask a set of questions designed to assess victims' risk level. The use of the risk indicator model by police officers involves professional discretion (Myhill & Johnstone, 2016) when research shows police misunderstanding of the dynamics of coercive control (Barlow, Johnstone, & Walklate, 2018; Myhill & Hohl, 2016; Robinson, Myhill, & Wire, 2018); the ramifications of this are explored further in Chapter Three. However, the increasingly shared language of risk paved the way for adoption of the Duluth model (Shepard & Pence, 1999; Gondolf, 2010) and the multi-agency risk assessment conference (MARAC), which started in Cardiff in 2003.[17]

Robinson and Tregidga (2007) identified the key components of multi-agency working as increased and ongoing communication, conducting a risk assessment, providing advocacy to victims, translating policy into action, and holding perpetrators to account. Adopting a common language of risk amongst agencies, the MARAC allows for the prioritisation of 'high-risk' victims (Robinson, 2006b). The MARAC facilitates discussion between key agencies (police, probation, health, child protection, housing, social work, prosecution, IDAA, and others) on options for increasing the safety of vulnerable victims and developing a coordinated action plan. Developed as part of a wider public protection response to violent and sexual crime, under the umbrella of the Multi-Agency Public Protection Arrangements ('MAPPA'), initial evaluation was positive (Robinson, 2004). It was found to improve information-sharing, inter-agency accountability, victim safety, and awareness about children (Robinson, 2006b).

MARAC research has observed the benefits of measuring risk (Hester & Westmarland, 2005) and managing safety, which has led to a roll-out across England and Wales and adoption of a similar model in Scotland. The model exploits existing research on the benefits of a coordinated, multi-agency approach (Rummery, 2013; Shepard & Pence, 1999), and there is evidence that potential benefits of the MARAC include reducing incidence of repeat victimisation, focussing limited resources effectively, assisting practitioners with a 'paper-trail' when a victim ceases to engage, and improving practitioner safety by identifying high-risk offenders (Robinson & Rowlands, 2009). Limitations of the MARAC were cited as victims' lack of cooperation and resources (Howarth & Robinson, 2016; Robinson & Howarth, 2012).

The MARAC has influenced policing, including the role of the Domestic Abuse Task Force in Scotland, a national proactive unit that targets repeat offenders. In England and Wales, the Crime and Security Act 2010 created Domestic Violence Protection Notices ('DVPNs') and Domestic Violence Protection Orders ('DVPOs'), which were rolled out across all police forces by 2014.[18] The Act gives police officers authority to serve perpetrators of domestic abuse with a DVPN, where they believe that a person is at risk of domestic violence. The notice is in place for 14–28 days to allow the police an opportunity to apply to the magistrate for a DVPOs. Police identification of risk of offending is informed by the multi-agency conferences.

Robinson (2006b) was right to highlight the benefits of innovative community responses, but risk management as a philosophy for tackling domestic abuse has developed in an ad hoc and reactive way. This supports calls for 'a more nuanced debate about the underlying rationale and associated goals of risk assessment in the policing context' (Ariza, Robinson, & Myhill, 2016, p. 347). There has been no government analysis of the practice of prioritising and managing cases based on a risk model, and the evolution of risk management to tackle domestic abuse has been relatively unchecked.

Development of the Risk Model: Disclosure and Review

Clare Wood was murdered by her ex-partner, George Appleton, shortly after she ended the relationship, when she was 36 years old. She was found strangled and burnt in her home in 2009. A police search for Appleton found him hanging in a derelict barn, where he had taken his own life. It subsequently emerged that Appleton had a record for violence against ex-partners and that Clare herself had made numerous reports to police between the end of the relationship and her death. Clare Wood's father and brother campaigned for a public register, so that those entering a relationship would have the right to find out about previous convictions for violence. Following the evidence of Clare's father at the inquest into her death, the Coroner recommended that men and women ought to be able to find out about their partner's criminal histories (Fitz-Gibbon & Walklate, 2017). On International Women's Day 2014, Clare's Law was rolled out across England and Wales, allowing police to disclose information about a partner's previous history of domestic violence or violent acts, following a formal application (Westmarland, 2015). It was not the first law to follow from a family campaign after the loss of loved ones. Sarah's Law provides a disclosure scheme to allow parents to find out if there is a convicted sex offender living in their area, following a campaign by the parents of murdered schoolgirl Sarah Payne in 2000. Both Sarah's Law and Clare's Law are an indication of the increasingly prominent profile of victims of crime (Garland, 2001).

Clare's Law was a positive initiative in England and Wales alongside national provision of DVPOs (Westmarland, 2015). However, in the same year, the Inspectorate of Constabulary published their report on police handling of domestic violence cases (HMIC, 2014)[19], which was highly critical of police practices. The report identified weaknesses in officer training, collection of evidence, and prioritisation of domestic abuse cases (Monckton-Smith, Williams, & Mullane, 2014).

Following the introduction of Clare's Law in England and Wales, the Disclosure Scheme for Domestic Abuse Scotland (DSDAS) was introduced in 2015 by the Domestic Abuse Task Force, a national police unit that supports the MARAC, identifies serial perpetrators and adopts a controversial, but effective, proactive model of policing. DSDAS encouraged victims to report ex-partners, even if they did not make a criminal complaint to the police during the abusive relationship. Thus, many police investigations became historic, which creates a barrier in obtaining best evidence. However, it is indicative of a wider understanding of domestic abuse and evidence of proactive policing. Further, combining multiple complainers and numerous charges has resulted in an increased number of cases being prosecuted before a jury or in the High Court and provides an opportunity for the court to sentence for cumulative offending.[20] Consequently, the work of the task force has been high-profile in Scotland, largely due to high-tariff sentences, including imprisonment and orders for lifelong restriction of liberty (Brown, 2016). The task force model was adapted from strategies used to tackle serial criminality.

In the Victim's Name – The Impact of Family Campaigns

The impact of Clare's law has been far reaching, but it is also an indictment of society's response: whilst the interests of the victim do not stand alone within the court process (Burton, 2008) and are still taken into account as part of the overall public interest test, there has been a shift in *emphasis* to give victims' views greater weight, largely due to cultural, policy, and legislative changes. In England and Wales and the United States, the victims' prominence has been influenced by 'a relationship between high-profile, emotive cases and subsequent criminal justice developments' (Duggan, 2018, p. 165). Other examples include Sarah's Law[21] and Megan's Law[22] (Duggan, 2018; Garland, 2001), which invoke a symbolic victim to legitimise more punitive measures (Hoyle, 2012).

In Scotland, there have been similar examples of high-profile family campaigns to affect change, but they have not translated into named laws in the same way. The campaign by the Dunblane families which led to reform of UK-wide firearms legislation within a year of the death of 16 children and their teacher in the classroom caused by a mass shooting is an obvious example.[23]

Stuart Drury is a name rote learned by law students in Scotland as a key case on provocation in murder trials (Chalmers & Leverick, 2012). His ex-partner, Marilyn McKenna, whom he was convicted of murdering, is less known. The trial did not focus on the domestic abuse or stalking experienced by the deceased.[24] However, Marilyn McKenna's death led to an overhaul of police recording in response to domestic abuse. Media reporting following her death included a BBC documentary that reported on a chilling telephone conversation between Marilyn and her sister where Marilyn predicted her own death (BBC, 2000). Predictable ought to be preventable. A review of police procedures led to an online vulnerable persons database (VPD). Crucially, the VPD allows police to track domestic incidents in different police areas and to identify repeat victimisation, even when cases do not result in a criminal prosecution. This measure reduces the ability of perpetrators to evade detection by repeatedly moving. Initially adopted by legacy Strathclyde Police, this was – by 2013 – rolled out across Police Scotland. The publicity around the retrial and documentary highlighted that Marilyn had been stalked, which contributed to efforts to introduce an offence of stalking,[25] delivered through the Criminal Justice and Licensing (Scotland) Act 2010.[26]

It seems that the influence of individuals and success of campaigns is largely impacted by the context of the day. The grassroots workers toiled for decades before achieving a platform from which they might be heard. Otherwise, individuals' influence appears to be dictated by a confluence of factors that are not wholly predictable and are often borne out of the tragedy of an idealised victim (Christie, 1986) or a relatable story. The distressing factor is that all of these legal reforms are in response to preventable deaths.

A Preventable Risk: Homicide Reviews

Introduced in England and Wales in 2011, a domestic homicide review (DHR) is a model of reviewing all murders by (ex)partners to chart a chronology of the circumstances leading to his/her death to identify if, and how, the death may have been prevented. Between 2011 and 2018, there were approximately 500 DHRs (Rowlands, 2019). DHRs will consider any help that a victim may have sought, interventions that were put in place or where an opportunity to identify risk and offer help was missed. They are a bold step by the government to acknowledge that many domestic homicides may be preventable. Introduced by the Domestic Violence Crime and Victims Act 2004,[27] their purpose is to: 'move toward identifying opportunities to prevent future homicide and forms part of the government's strategy to end violence against women and girls'. Specifically, chronologies and temporal sequences are potentially useful in understanding the dynamic nature of risk, and how and when it can escalate (Monckton-Smith, 2021).

Beyond the government's analysis of its own data, Ingala Smith[28] has developed the *Counting Dead Women* database, which records 575 homicides where women were killed by men between 2012 and 2015. Of those, 372 were domestic homicides. Following analysis of these deaths, Monckton-Smith (2021) has developed a homicide timeline which breaks each abusive relationship into eight common steps and provides a compelling analysis of how domestic homicides are preventable. Other countries to adopt versions of a DHR include Australia, Canada, New Zealand, the United States, Portugal, and Northern Ireland (Rowlands, 2019).[29]

There is currently no DHR in Scotland, although there is a commitment within the *Equally Safe* delivery plan (Scottish Government, 2017b).

IV: DEVELOPING GENDERED POLICIES

Both Scotland and England and Wales have introduced policies that represent a commitment to recognise domestic abuse within a broader umbrella of violence against women and girls and to categorise it as gendered offending. The language of these policies suggests they have been influenced by the Istanbul Convention[30] that identifies four pillars to combat violence against women and girls (prevention, protection, prosecution, and coordinated policies) and posits domestic abuse as gendered violence.

UK-wide policies are the result of enduring commitment from the third-sector, academic research, and improved public awareness. In this section, we will look at the current policies, how they have influenced professional training and how they have set the bar for a high expectation of a gendered policy approach within the neutrality of the law.

Both jurisdictions adopt a gender-neutral definition of domestic abuse within a gendered policy understanding of abuse. This means that the law recognises that anyone can perpetrate a crime of domestic abuse and anyone can be a victim, whilst the government also recognises that the most serious and pernicious offences of coercively controlling domestic abuse are predominantly perpetrated by men on women within heterosexual relationships (Hester, 2013). Thus, whilst the law remains neutral in its definition of the crime, the policy that supports the law is gendered. The policies in both jurisdictions recognise the vulnerability of women to this type of offending and ensure that their policy reflects that.

The *Violence Against Women and Girls Strategy*, England and Wales

Government policy on domestic abuse is encompassed in a wider strategy on *Violence Against Women and Girls Strategy, 2016–2020* (HM Government, 2016) that consolidated their original policy on gender based violence (GBV) *Our Call to End Violence Against Women and Girls* (HM Government, 2010). It is a policy that encapsulates sexual violence, stalking, honour-based crimes, domestic abuse, forced genital mutilation, and forced marriage.

The current policy retains the key 'pillars' set down in 2010 of prevention, provision of services, partnership working, and pursuing perpetrators. It aims to *prevent* GBV through an extended education programme in schools to promote healthy relationships and teach teenagers about consent. It commits to increased service *provision* for rape crisis centres, refuges, and support agencies but introduces a National Statement of Expectations to set core expectations and a benchmark for *partnerships* on adopting best practice but recognising differing local needs. Thus, the provision of services was intrinsically linked to the government expectation of partnership working as an ongoing commitment: access to funds appears to be predicated on meeting standards. In relation to *pursuing perpetrators*, it is encouraging that the policy recognises the need to tackle patterns of abuse and edge away from an incident-focused approach. However, where there could have been greater commitment to bespoke perpetrator programmes, the spotlight was on the use of technology and 'smart' responses, such as greater use of electronic tagging.[31]

The strategy is translated into practice by the Domestic Abuse Best Practice Framework and a National Delivery Group, attended by the Crown Prosecution Service (CPS) lead for Domestic Abuse, the Commissioner,[32] and key criminal justice agencies and support agencies involved in the multi-agency response.[33] The strategy is regularly revised and is due to be refreshed in 2021;

whilst it is anticipated that it will continue to consolidate existing policy, it is likely to specifically tackle online abuse such as cyber flashing (McGlynn & Johnson, 2021), intimate image abuse (McGlynn et al., 2020), and 'upskirting' (McGlynn, Rackley, & Houghton, 2017). The Government consultation on their 2021-2024 strategy has recognised that:

> *the risks of violence against women and girls that existed 10 years ago are still present, but the pace of societal and technological change means that new and evolving forms of crimes against women and girls are continuously emerging. A new Violence Against Women and Girls Strategy is required to ensure that these crimes are tackled effectively.*[34]

The consultation on a new policy completed early 2020. A separate position statement on government policy relating to male victims of sexual violence and domestic abuse was published in 2019. Whilst it is refreshingly honest in the limitations of its understanding of the complex dynamics of male victimisation – the data are largely quantitative analysis of the crime survey – it does not acknowledge the impact of non-recent institutional abuse. Nevertheless, the discrete impact of sexual and domestic abuse on masculinity is under-acknowledged, and the government recognition of structural, cultural, and individual barriers is progressive. Disappointingly, there is no similar policy in Scotland, although there is a useful acknowledgement of challenges to masculinity within the Scottish policy on violence against women, *Equally Safe*.[35]

Equally Safe, Scotland

The Scottish approach has also developed from specific policies on domestic abuse to wider policies encompassing all aspects of gendered violence against women and girls.

The publication of *Equally Safe* (2014, 2016c) represented a commitment from the government to recognise domestic abuse within a broader umbrella of violence against women and girls and to categorise it as gendered offending. This approach was nudged forward by *Safer Lives, Changed Lives* in 2009. In 2010, a short policy think piece titled *What does gender have to do with violence against women?* was published to complement the 2009 strategy. It was the first Scottish recognition of domestic abuse as part of the wider dimension of violence against women and situated domestic abuse as a predominantly gendered problem. Its goal was to spell out the link between gender equality and violence against women and paved the way for the approach in *Equally Safe*. Like policy in England and Wales, it built on earlier strategies and retained the overlapping but distinct '4 Ps' of prevention, protection, provision, and participation. Its aim is to: 'work collaboratively with key partners in the public, private and third sectors to prevent and eradicate all forms of violence against women and girls'. It echoes the commitment of the UN Convention[36] and adopts a rights-based approach. Similar to England and Wales, the focus is on education.

The definition of violence against women is wider than in England, where commercial sexual exploitation or prostitution is not included. *Equally Safe* defines violence against women and girls as encompassing (but not limited to):

> *physical, sexual and psychological violence occurring in the family (including children and young people), within the general community or in institutions, including domestic abuse, rape, and incest; sexual harassment, bullying and intimidation in any public or private space, including work; commercial sexual exploitation, including prostitution, lap dancing, stripping, pornography and trafficking; child sexual*

> *abuse, including familial sexual abuse, child sexual exploitation and online abuse; so called 'honour based' violence, including dowry related violence, female genital mutilation, forced and child marriages, and 'honour' crimes.*[37]

In both England and Wales and Scotland, the strategies were augmented by expert boards to ensure implementation and complemented by funding commitments for grassroots services. However, there is no published evaluation of their utility: what do they achieve? Whilst they may seem aspirational, the governments' commitments offer promising capstone policies within which to consider more meaningful ways of recognising domestic abuse as gendered offending and, crucially, led to increased funding to train professionals and facilitate multi-agency working. Moreover, in both jurisdictions, their key commitments have been translated into published Codes for Victims (Home Office 2005, 2021; Scottish Government, 2015, 2020).

Thus, whilst gendered policies may appear contradictory and problematic, they ought to be seen as a nuanced understanding which recognises the gendered dynamic of domestic abuse within the neutrality and universality of the law.

CONCLUSION

This chapter illustrates the significant changes that have taken place to recognise and respond to domestic abuse. Much has happened since devolution and the Human Rights Act, but this was grounded in efforts since the 1970s and a committed grassroots campaign and second-wave feminism (Davies, 2011). Policies have shown consistent intent to deal with violence against women, specifically domestic abuse, and support vulnerable victims. The campaigners and policy development have framed the criminal justice response and set the scene for legislative development: how this unfolded is described in Chapter Two.

NOTES

1. On the early policing response, see Dobash and Dobash (1979), S. Edwards (1989), and Walker (1979).

2. Marion Blythman, founding member of Edinburgh Women's Aid, in an interview with *Speaking Out: An Oral History of Scottish Women's Aid* (Scottish Women's Aid, 2017).

3. Still an annual event. Visit: http://www.reclaimthenight.co.uk/.

4. It also called for governments to administer compensation schemes and for financial restitution to form part of sentencing, but the UK had been administering the Criminal Injuries Compensation Authority (CICA) since 1964, to provide compensation to victims of crime.

5. Their most high-profile success was a campaign of support for Sally Challen whose conviction for the murder of her husband was reduced to manslaughter on appeal, as it was recognised that she had been a victim of coercively controlling behaviour at the time. For further information, visit: wwwjusticeforwomen.org.uk.

6. For further information, visit: www.engender.org.uk.

7. Article 3.

8. Article 8.

9. See Home Page|Equality and Human Rights Commission (equalityhumanrights.com)

10. For critique, see Burton's (2008) and Hoyle's (2011) findings on retraction rates despite a multi-agency response.

11. In England and Wales, roll out of 25 SDVCs in 2006 but none since. In Scotland, there are two specialist courts (Glasgow and

Edinburgh) and four cluster courts (Ayr, Livingston, Dunfermline, and Falkirk).

12. Citizens Advice Bureau, COPFS, Families Outside (a charity to support families of the imprisoned), Highland Council Criminal Justice Social Work, Social Security and Child Support Tribunal, Employment Tribunal, NHS Highland, Police Scotland, Scottish Women's Aid, and Witness Service/Victim Support Scotland.

13. In England and Wales, the Ministry of Justice (2020) favours greater specialism, and in Scotland, the Equally Safe Delivery Plan (Scottish Government, 2017b) commits to specialist domestic abuse courts.

14. Formerly Coordinated Action Against Domestic Abuse (CAADA), it is a UK-wide charity founded by Dianna Barren in 2005 to end domestic abuse. Further information can be found at: http://www.safelives.org.uk/about-us/our-history-and-impact.

15. https://www.cps.gov.uk/domestic-abuse-cps-programme-2020-2021.

16. Now referred to as the Dash Risk Checklist in England and Wales and the Risk Indicator Checklist (RIC) in Scotland.

17. For an overview of how MARACs work, see CAADA (2010).

18. Now incorporated into the Domestic Abuse Act 2021; see Chapter Two.

19. In England and Wales, independent inspections are carried out jointly by HMCPSI (Her Majesty's Crown Prosecution Service Inspectorate) and HMICFRS (Her Majesty's Inspectorate of Constabulary and Fire & Rescue Services, formerly HMIC (Her Majesty's Inspectorate of Constabulary): relevant reports include HMCPSI and HMICFRS, 2020 and HMIC, 2014. In Scotland, independent inspections on the police response to domestic abuse were carried out by HMICS (Her Majesty's Inspectorate of Constabulary Scotland): see HMICS, 1997; 2008. See also Joint Thematic Report with Her Majesty's Inspectorate of Prosecutions, Scotland on responses to victims (2010; 2011).

20. Multiple charge of similar facts, character and circumstance can prove in Scots law by virtue of the doctrine of mutual

corroboration, known as the Moorov Doctrine. For a fuller explanation see Ross and Chalmers (1201, para. 5-10).

21. A sexual offences register was introduced in England and Wales, under the name Sarah's Law, after murdered Sarah Payne.

22. In the United States, the sexual offences register is named Megan's Law, after murdered Megan Kanka.

23. Firearms Amendment Act 1997.

24. This decision was rewritten as part of the Scottish Feminist Judgement Project (Cowan, Kennedy, & Munro, 2019); see further discussion in Chapter Six.

25. For further information on the wider campaign by Ann Moulds to recognise stalking as a specific offence, see: www.actionagainststalking.org.

26. s39.

27. s9: the Act did not come into force until 2014, although there was operation of DHRs from 2011.

28. For further information, visit: Counting Dead Women|aKaren Ingala Smith

29. For a discussion of the application of these models, see Rowlands (2019). For an overview of the operation of DHRs in England and Wales, see Monckton-Smith (2021).

30. Council of Europe Convention on Preventing and Combating Violence Against Women and Domestic Violence (Istanbul Convention), ratified 2011.

31. For a discussion on the merits of electronic monitoring, see Graham and McIvor (2017); for an overview of modes of electronic monitoring and an evaluation of practice in Scotland, see Scottish Government (2019).

32. The role of Commissioner for Domestic Abuse is introduced by the Domestic Abuse Act 2021, s4. For further information, visit: https://www.gov.uk/government/publications/domestic-abuse-bill-2020-factsheets/domestic-abuse-commissioner-factsheet.

33. For further information, visit: https://www.cps.gov.uk/domestic-abuse-cps-programme-2020-2021.

34. HM Government (2020) Violence Against Women Strategy, Call for Evidence, Executive Summary, retrieved at: Violence Against Women and Girls (VAWG) strategy 2021 to 2024: call for evidence - GOV.UK (www.gov.uk)

35. Scottish Government (2018, p. 20): 'A gendered analysis does not exclude men, but rather recognises that women and girls are disproportionately affected by particular forms of violence that they experience because they are women and girls. The prevailing societal view of what constitutes masculinity makes it difficult for men to identify themselves as experiencing abuse and can prevent them from seeking help. Gay and bisexual men and boys experience violence and abuse that also targets their sexual orientation. More fundamentally, masculinity and femininity are part of the underlying social construct of gender that contributes to the continuing prevalence of violence against women and girls in society'.

36. CEDAW (1979): it has been signed but not ratified by the UK. Available at: OHCHR|Convention on the Elimination of All Forms of Discrimination against Women.

37. *Equally Safe* (2014, 2016).

Chapter Two

LAW*

INTRODUCTION

Whilst policies in relation to domestic abuse have followed similar paths across the UK, the law in England and Wales is different from the law in Scotland. Both share a common law, adversarial heritage, distinct from European inquisitorial systems (Jackson & Summers, 2012). However, there has traditionally been more legislative reform in England and Wales, whereas Scots law has developed through the precedent of judicial decisions. Pre-devolution, the 'Westminster drag' (Charles & Mackay, 2013, p. 602) was recognised as a barrier to reform of Scots law. Distinct legislation relating to Scotland was rare; a chapter at the bottom of English statute was more likely. Post-devolution, despite a vigorous legislative programme (Chalmers & Leverick, 2013), the opportunity to craft tailor-made, responsive legislation and engage communities in the creation of welfare policies has not been fully exploited (McAra, 2008; Mooney & Scott, 2005) with copycat policies and pro-forma legislation (Croall, 2005) from England and

---

*All primary legislation can be accessed online at: www.opsi.gov.uk.

Wales. The Scottish government may seem to have followed the Westminster lead on some recent policy and legislation, but there are other examples of Scotland setting the agenda. The creation of offences through statute, rather than evolution of the common law, is also influenced by the European Union (EU) (Jackson & Summers, 2012). Since devolution and since the Human Rights Act 1998, both jurisdictions have consistently taken the opportunity to implement legislation to protect against gender-based violence and to promote victims' rights.

In this chapter, the laws of each jurisdiction are narrated separately. The purpose is not to compare but to provide a basic synopsis of key provisions of civil and criminal law that relate to victims, specifically victims of domestic abuse. Qualitative research with victims about their experience of court and accessing justice illustrates that victims make no distinction between civil and criminal procedures and that two concurrent processes are a potential barrier to justice (Burton, 2008; Cook et al., 2004; Forbes, 2018; Robinson, 2007). The consequences and opportunities inherent in this finding are explored in Chapter Six. The purpose of this chapter is to highlight key provisions in:

- *English criminal law* that protects victims (of domestic abuse).
- *English civil law* that protects victims (of domestic abuse).
- *Scottish criminal law* that protects victims (of domestic abuse).
- *Scottish civil law* that protects victims (of domestic abuse).

UN AND EU INFLUENCE

Both jurisdictions have been influenced by UN conventions and EU law, although these are sometimes translated differently.

The Istanbul Convention[1] was introduced in 2011 and aims to prevent and combat violence against women, specifically domestic abuse, providing a legal framework for third-sector agencies to hold government to account in relation to funding of services. It frames domestic abuse as a human rights violation. There has been a concerted campaign by feminist activists, seeking to persuade the UK government to ratify the convention. Whilst the UK became a signatory in 2012, it has still to be ratified.[2]

The EU Directive on Victims' Rights 2012[3] sets out minimum standards on the treatment and rights of victims. It includes the right to information, fair treatment, access to justice, reparation, and protection from secondary victimisation. The directive is implemented differently across member states. In the UK, the Criminal Injuries Compensation Authority (CICA) already provided reparation to victims (Rock, 2004) so that the focus was on the provision of information and protective measures to support attendance at court. Both jurisdictions implemented Victim Charters and Codes of Practice for Victims, to meet the standards. In Scotland, it led to the Victims and Witnesses (Scotland) Act 2014, whereas in England and Wales, amendments were made to the Domestic Violence, Crime and Victims Act 2004.

Civil Law in England and Wales

In England and Wales, there was a hierarchy of provision,[4] until the Matrimonial Homes Act 1983. This was not legislation introduced specifically to address domestic abuse, but it 'became the principle legislation governing court orders' (Burton, 2008, p.12). The legislation set out relevant factors for the court to consider in granting wives a right of occupation. Judicial interpretation of these factors was varied and, in

1992, the Law Commission identified gaps in the legislation and disparity in its application (Burton, 2008). As a result, the law was consolidated by the Family Law Act 1996 when all courts were granted jurisdiction to consider injunctions, non-molestation orders, and protective orders. Whilst this legislation was welcome, research found little differentiation between the granting and enforcement of injunctions before and after the introduction of the Act (I. Edwards, 2004). The financial burden of raising a civil case was a key barrier. Burton (2008) points out that changes to law do not always invite developments in practice, and I. Edwards (2004) also found that judges tolerated multiple breaches of an injunction before enforcing a penalty.

The Protection from Harassment Act 1997 created an offence of harassment,[5] which is described in the Act as a course of conduct. The legislation also has sections relevant to Scotland (discussed below). The 1997 Act blurred the traditional divide between civil and criminal court jurisdictions because it created a criminal offence of breaching a civil order.[6] Despite some speculation, it did not result in the civil courts applying a more stringent burden of proof[7] (Burton, 2008). The Domestic Violence Crimes and Victims Act 2004 was the first English legislation to specifically address domestic abuse and brought in wide and varied provision. The Act made amendments to the Family Law Act 1996 to make breach of a non-molestation order a criminal offence[8] and extended the categories of parties eligible to apply for occupation orders and non-molestation orders: it was open to those in same-sex relationships[9] and those not cohabiting[10] to apply to the court for protection. Unusually, the Act allows the court to impose a restraining order in the event of an acquittal following a criminal trial, but this was not implemented into law until 2009.[11]

The Civil Procedure (Amendment) Rules 2021 provide statutory protective measures for vulnerable witnesses in the civil court, for the first time. *Re W [2010] UKSC 12* overturned the presumption that children should not give evidence in civil proceedings and has been the leading authority for the general provision that a child or vulnerable witness is entitled to protective measures in the civil court, as directed by the judge, if they are necessary to ensure fair questioning of the witness and that proceedings are 'just' (for a discussion of the case, see Brammer and Cooper, 2011). Nevertheless, this relies on solicitors recognising vulnerability and making appropriate applications (Gold, 2021). Constrained eligibility for legal aid has increased the number of party litigants, which is problematic in cases of domestic abuse, as it is inappropriate for an abuser to question his victim directly and vulnerability is less likely to be recognised. However, this has been remedied by the Domestic Abuse Act 2021.[12] The 2021 Act strengthens the availability of special measures: in the family court, where there is evidence of domestic abuse, the judge must assume vulnerability and make an order for appropriate special measures;[13] in the civil court, where there is evidence of domestic abuse, the judge must consider the vulnerability of the victim and the impact that vulnerability has on their ability to be party to proceedings.[14]

The use of special measures is established (if underused) in the family court, but their use in the civil court has been reinforced by Practice Direction 1A,[15] following recommendations of the Civil Justice Council[16] in their 2020 report. The provisions mirror civil practice in Northern Ireland and Scotland and allow parties to apply to the court for protective measures. Disappointingly, the report adopts the misapprehension that: 'generally speaking a criminal court will often be a more intimidating environment for a vulnerable witness than a civil or family court'. Moreover, in mimicking the provisions in Scotland and Northern Ireland, an opportunity was lost to re-evaluate what it means for witnesses attending civil court hearings and the need for greater support at an earlier stage in the process. This is explored in the following chapters.

Criminal Law in England and Wales

The Domestic Abuse Act 2021 created a specific offence of domestic abuse. It also consolidated and extended many procedural rights for victims. Prior to the 2021 Act, prosecutors relied on the common law and statute to select the most appropriate charge. Nevertheless, some legislative changes addressed aspects of the criminal law.[17]

The first piece of modern legislation to specifically tackle domestic abuse was the Domestic Violence, Crime and Victims Act 2004. It introduced the Victim Commissioner[18] whose function is to promote the interests of victims[19] and monitor application of the Code of Practice for Victims of Crime.[20] The Commissioner fulfils an institutional advocacy role on behalf of victims, where collective issues are identified, rather than representing individual victim's issues. The 2004 Act also created an offence of domestic homicide.[21] Further, it made common assault in England and Wales an arrestable offence[22] (it has always been an arrestable offence in Scotland). In creating a new offence of domestic homicide, the Act also created domestic homicide reviews – a mechanism whereby an independent review is conducted of each domestic homicide (discussed in Chapter One).

In 2013, the Criminal Practice Direction[23] introduced the concept of ground rules hearings for cases involving a vulnerable witness or a vulnerable accused. This is a hearing between the initial bail hearing and trial to set ground rules about how witnesses can be questioned and what protective measures are needed to ensure witnesses give their 'best evidence' but also to protect the rights of the accused. The ground rules hearings were introduced at the same time as intermediaries (Cooper, Backen, & Marchant, 2017). Distinct from the limited role of the support person in Scotland or the statutory provision for Evidence by Commissioner,[24] an intermediary ensures that the witness understands the questions. Where an intermediary is appointed for a child or vulnerable witness, (s)he provides written guidance to relevant lawyers or barristers about the witness' level of understanding and advises on how to frame simple questions. Research shows that intermediaries not only translate the language of the court to simplify questions for children and complainants of sexual abuse, they can also reduce the worry of attending court and improve confidence (Cooper & Mattison, 2017). Their report is placed before the court at the ground rules hearing and parties agree on the parameters of questions. During the trial, the intermediary will only intervene if (s)he considers that the witness has not understood a question or has been misled. This is a much stronger protection for vulnerable witnesses than the role of a supporter who is no more than a comforting and familiar face[25] in the courtroom, unable to speak or interject.

Protective special measures were introduced by the Youth Justice Criminal Evidence Act 1999, which allowed the prosecutor to apply to the court for a range of measures, where the court was persuaded of vulnerability. Those measures are wider than in the civil court and include screens,[26] evidence via TV link,[27] evidence in private,[28] the removal of wigs and gowns,[29] the option to pre-record evidence in chief,[30] an intermediary to assist them give evidence,[31] and aids to communication.[32] The 2021 Act adds victims of domestic abuse to the categories of victim 'deemed vulnerable'[33] and eligible for special measures.[34]

The Serious Crime Act 2015 introduced an offence[35] of coercive control.[36] The Act created an offence of coercive or controlling behaviour in a family relationship. An offence is constituted by repeatedly or continuously engaging in behaviour that is controlling or coercive.[37] Like harassment and stalking offences, it is a course of conduct.[38] Whilst designed to tackle domestic abuse, it is wider than intimate partner relationships and extends to other family members in the same family[39] but cannot be perpetrated against a child.[40] The behaviour must have a 'serious effect'[41] on the victim that is defined as causing fear on at least two occasions[42] or causing serious alarm or distress which has a substantial adverse effect on the victim's usual day-to-day activities.[43] A test of *reasonableness* is applied.[44] The offence of coercive control is statutory recognition of the often psychological nature of domestic abuse, but it does not cover the spectrum of offending behaviours. The reasonableness test (also adopted in Scotland) is problematic and has unintended consequences for victims (Forbes, 2018), as discussed in Chapter Six. There has been a mixed response to the criminalisation of domestic abuse as coercive control (see discussion below), but it has been the precursor to a specific offence of domestic abuse.

Following the introduction of a specific offence of domestic abuse in Scotland in 2018, the Home Office consulted on a specific offence. The Domestic Abuse Bill had a stuttering start and was unable to progress through Parliament in 2019 due to dissolution for a general election and restrictions necessitated by a global Covid-19 pandemic. It received Royal Assent in April 2021 and creates an offence of domestic abuse, defined as abusive behaviour of a person A towards a person B if both are aged 16 years or over and 'personally connected'. Abusive behaviour is defined as:

(a) physical or sexual abuse;

(b) violent or threatening behaviour;

(c) controlling or coercive behaviour;

(d) economic abuse; and

(e) psychological, emotional or other abuse.[45]

The legislation does not distinguish between single incidents and a course of conduct and defines economic abuse as behaviour that 'has a substantial adverse effect on B's ability to (a) acquire, use or maintain money or other property, or (b) obtain goods or services'.[46] The Act defines 'personally connected' widely to include parental and familial relationships, not just intimate partner relationships. This is distinct from the Scottish definition. The legislation deems any abuse against a child of the household as abuse of B.

The 2021 Act also creates an offence of non-fatal strangulation.[47] This underscores the existing general proposition that a person may not consent to the infliction of serious harm and, by extension, is unable to consent to their own death (this is aimed to tackle the so-called rough sex defence)[48] and extends the current offence of coercively controlling behaviour to ex-partners.[49]

Beyond criminality, the 2021 Act introduces and extends various safety measures and procedural rights, including establishing in law the office of Domestic Abuse Commissioner;[50] extending protection notices and orders;[51] placing a duty on local authorities to provide support to victims of domestic abuse and their children in refuges and other safe accommodation;[52] prohibiting perpetrators of abuse from cross-examining their victims in person in the civil and family courts;[53] creating a statutory presumption that victims of domestic abuse are eligible for special measures in the criminal and family courts;[54] extending the extraterritorial jurisdiction of the criminal courts in England and Wales, Scotland, and Northern Ireland to further violent and sexual offences;[55] providing for polygraph testing as a condition of licence on release from custody;[56] enshrining the disclosure scheme ('Clare's Law') in statute;[57] placing a statutory duty on local authorities to protect victims of domestic abuse and their children at contact centres;[58] and stating that those homeless as a result of fleeing abuse will automatically have 'priority need' for homelessness assistance and protections in relation to secure tenancies.[59]

SafeLives and other charities welcomed the Act but fear an opportunity has been missed during the legislative process to place a statutory *obligation* on local authorities to provide refuge and community support to victims and have criticised the government for not protecting migrant women with no recourse to public funds (*SafeLives*, 2021). Currently, refuge provision is inconsistent across the UK, and there is insufficient safe housing for women and children fleeing abuse (Grierson, 2018; *SafeLives*, 2021)[60] and cuts to women's services (Towers & Walby, 2012). Questions have been raised about the merit of criminalisation and more law (see discussion below), but this Act arguably redefines the gold standard as the most comprehensive, legislative package as it includes not only a specific offence of domestic abuse but procedural protections for victims *throughout* the process.

Civil Law in Scotland

Scotland has a rich common law heritage, including interdict. The first legislative protection for intimate partners was the Matrimonial Homes (Family Protection) (Scotland) Act 1981 that allowed (un)married women to have an abusive partner excluded from the matrimonial home. Protective orders included an exclusion order, but it was only effective if combined with an ancillary order,[61] such as an order for ejection (Hughes, 2011). Research has shown that exclusion orders are underused, representing just over 1% of family court work and mostly upholding the status quo occupancy of the home (Dickson, Jackson, Laing, & Rosengard, 2010). A mandatory power of arrest was attached to the orders by an amendment to the legislation in 2001.[62] It was not until the Civil Partnership Act 2004 that remedies under the 1981 Act were accessible to those in a same-sex relationship.

The Protection from Harassment Act 1997 recognised the right to be free from harassment as a course of conduct and introduced the remedies of award of damages or interdict.[63] It also created a criminal offence of being in breach of a non-harassment order (NHO). The Protection from Abuse (Scotland) Act 2001 allowed power of arrest to be attached to any kind of interdict and specifically introduced domestic interdicts. The Domestic Abuse (Scotland) Act 2011 was the first legislation specifically designed to protect victims of domestic abuse, and section 8A was inserted into the 1997 Act to recognise harassment as domestic abuse.

Child residence and contact is governed by the Children (Scotland) Act 1995.[64] In England and Wales, this is governed by the Children Act 1989.[65] Key to consideration of a child's welfare is their view (J. Thomson, 2014).[66] The statutory presumption that a child 12 years or older may give their views will be removed when the Children (Scotland) Act 2020[67] comes into force and the courts are already adopting the new policy that any child may be able to provide his/her view.[68] There is no checklist in Scotland of what constitutes the best interests of the child (Sutherland, 2018), but s11(7A)–(7E)[69] provides that the court must take into account the need to protect child(ren) from abuse or the threat of abuse which *might* affect them, the ability of a person who has carried out abuse to care for the child, and the effect any (risk of) abuse might have on another person with parental responsibilities.[70] Unfortunately, research suggests a lack of understanding and under use of this provision by solicitors (Whitecross, 2017).

Whilst developments provide more remedies for those in abusive relationships, barriers remain. Civil remedies for domestic abuse are inherently problematic as they may contribute to the unhelpful rhetoric that not all abuse is criminal. Service of civil papers can be understood as the start of a conversation. If a woman has successfully removed herself from a dangerous environment, or the perpetrator has left the home, she may not want to start such a conversation: like leaving in the first instance, the service of legal papers may be an inflammatory risk factor. Financial concern is also key. There is little accurate information about eligibility for legal aid: many women are not eligible, some do not seek advice because they believe they would not be eligible, and others who are eligible still have to pay a proportion of the fee. The legal aid rules arguably act as a disincentive to solicitors who may consider that an interdict is not worth pursuing. Civil remedies are seen as a costly risk factor for victims and solicitors alike.

Protective measures in Scotland are called special measures and are governed by the Vulnerable Witnesses (Scotland) Act 2004, as amended by the Victims and Witnesses Scotland Act 2014.[71] In civil proceedings, similar to England and Wales, parties can apply to the court for special measures in advance of proof. Measures include taking of evidence by Commissioner,[72] use of a live television link in accordance,[73] use of screen,[74] use of a supporter,[75] or any other measures that the Scottish ministers may, by order made by statutory instrument, prescribe.[76]

Criminal Law in Scotland

The Domestic Abuse (Scotland) Act 2018 was groundbreaking legislation that created a specific offence of domestic abuse for the first time. Previously, offences amounting to domestic abuse were prosecuted under a wide range of common law and statutory offences. Akin to England and Wales, offences were 'flagged' as being domestic abuse by the inclusion of a domestic abuse aggravator. This practice evolved to allow police and prosecutors to count the number of domestic abuse cases to grasp the scale of the problem and to respond to Freedom of Information requests.[77] It also allowed police and prosecutors to identify repeat, analogous offending. From the accused's point of view, however, it was a dubious practice, untested by solicitors. This has recently been partly remedied by the introduction of a statutory aggravator,[78] where the Crown requires to prove, by a single source, the aggravation and thereafter the aggravation must be taken into account during sentencing.

Whilst any crime known to the law of Scotland could be aggravated as being 'domestic abuse', in practice, the majority of charges related to physical assaults, shouting, and swearing. Since the introduction of an offence of stalking in 2010,[79] a significant proportion of those offences are aggravated by being domestic abuse, and it provided a limited opportunity to criminally recognise some behaviour as a course of conduct. Appeal Court decisions requiring a public element or 'discoverability' to breach of the peace (broadly similar to affray in England and Wales) have inevitably led to a reduction in its use for domestic abuse, and contraventions of the Criminal Law (Consolidation) (Scotland) Act 2010, section 38, are more commonly charged (Ferguson & McDiarmid, 2014). This makes it an offence to behave in a threatening or abusive manner, likely to place an individual in a state of fear and alarm. Such an offence benefits from being an objective test and, accurately libelled, has some scope to reflect a course of conduct.

The Protection from Harassment Act 1997 (discussed above) allowed the prosecutor to ask the court to consider granting an NHO, following conviction, if the crime related to harassment.[80] There has been little research on the extent to which prosecutors sought NHOs and the extent to which sheriffs imposed them. The Domestic Abuse (Scotland) Act 2018 made it mandatory for sheriffs and judges to consider an NHO where there is a conviction for domestic abuse,[81] irrespective of a motion by the prosecutor. Where no NHO is imposed, the judge must give reasons. This is a significant shift that fits with the provision made in the 2018 Act to ensure that victim safety is a material consideration in sentencing[82] and is being robustly enforced by the Sheriff Appeal Court.[83]

The Victims and Witnesses (Scotland) Act 2014 was the first legal recognition of 'victims' (rather than complainers or witnesses) in Scotland. It purports to engage greater participatory rights to victims, including the automatic grant of special measures,[84] the right to determine the gender of a medical practitioner in cases of serious sexual assault,[85] and the right to an interpreter.[86] It creates categories of 'deemed vulnerable' witnesses who are automatically entitled to special measures within the courtroom. Encouragingly, for England and Wales, who have just implemented a similar presumptive right to protective measures in the Domestic Abuse Act 2020, the 2014 Act in Scotland led to an increase in the use of special measures (Carloway, 2015) and it introduced two shifts towards greater consultee rights: first, the right to make representations post-conviction in relation to release from prison on licence[87] and in relation to conditions attaching to the terms of an temporary release;[88] and second, the review of a decision not to prosecute[89] (the 'Victims' Right to Review').

Scotland became the first jurisdiction to introduce a specific offence of domestic abuse. Dubbed the 'gold standard' by Evan Stark and "fundamentally innovative"[90] by SWA CEO, Dr Marsha Scott, The Domestic abuse (Scotland) Act 2018 created a specific offence, in section 1, of domestic abuse by engaging in a course of violent,[91] threatening or intimidating behaviour that is abusive towards a partner or ex-partner.[92] Section 4 creates an aggravation where behaviour is directed towards a child or involves a child in the commission of the offence.[93] The accused is prohibited from conducting his own defence and unable to cross-examine the victim directly.[94] The Act makes it possible to prosecute physical *and/or* emotional abuse as one, continuing offence. Section 2 provides the relevant effects of behaviour which will be criminalised:

(a) making B dependent on, or subordinate to, A;

(b) isolating B from friends, relatives, or other sources of support;

(c) controlling, regulating, or monitoring B's day-to-day activities;

(d) depriving B of, or restricting B's, freedom of action; and

(e) frightening, humiliating, degrading, or punishing B.[95]

The novel aspect of the legislation is the introduction of behaviours which relate to psychological and emotional abuse and are understood as 'coercive control' (Stark, 2007). The rationale for recognising all abusive behaviours in one criminal charge is an understanding of gendered experiences of a continuum of abuse, rather than being incident focussed.

Despite the initiative of the 2018 Act, the pre-existence of the procedural rights contained in the Victims and Witnesses (Scotland) Act 2014 Act meant that the 2018 Act had a single focus and did not provide the umbrella legislation for domestic abuse that is created by the Domestic Abuse Act 2021 in England and Wales. Some gaps in legislation in Scotland have been filled by the Vulnerable Witnesses (Criminal Evidence) (Scotland) Act 2019 which allows for Evidence by Commissioner[96] and the Domestic Abuse (Protection) (Scotland) Act

2021 which provides for domestic abuse protection notices and orders.[97] The Evidence and Procedure Review (Dorrian, 2021) noted the improvements from greater use of commissions and the benefit of more detailed case management by preliminary hearing judges, including the adoption of ground rules hearings.

Alongside the introduction of protective measures in England and Wales, both a Victims' Commissioner and a Commissioner for Domestic Abuse have been introduced to ensure implementation of service rights for victims and to campaign for further reform. In Scotland, whilst there is a Procurator Fiscal for Domestic Abuse, acting in the public interest as a prosecutor, there is no Commissioner.[98] With a single police force in Scotland and a relatively small jurisdiction with a strong multi-agency network, the case for Commissioners has not yet been made. Nevertheless, within the context of women's mixed experiences and resounding feelings of remaining unheard, the benefits of a Commissioner to lend voice to a disenfranchised group are persuasive.

CIVIL REMEDY?

A main critique of the civil courts is the lack of procedural protections for victims attending court. Protective measures designed for criminal trials have been transposed into civil rules to provide some protection at the stage of proof. However, just as few criminal cases result in trial, even fewer civil cases result in proof. The key difference is that parties are not required to attend the procedural hearing in a criminal case. There is a public prosecutor and a defence solicitor or barrister: it is not the victim's case but a prosecution in the public interest. In the civil court, the victim is party to proceedings and attends the procedural hearings. At these early stages of a child welfare hearing, there are no protective measures: the courtroom is configured to be more convivial than the adversarial formality of the criminal court. Whilst this is helpful in many cases, it is inappropriate for victims of domestic abuse to wait in the same corridor as their abuser, sit across a small table, and be questioned directly. Constraints on legal aid provision combined with increased financial abuse throughout the court process compound these difficulties. Thus, whilst civil remedies have adapted and developed to tackle domestic abuse and offer protective measures to victims, there are barriers to fully exploiting their benefits. This is explored in Chapter Three.

IS MORE LAW THE ANSWER?[99]

The criminalisation thesis is not new (Lacey, 2007, 2016) and is relevant to the public prosecution of intimate partner relationships (for a synopsis of the debate, see Walklate & Fitz-Gibbon, 2021). The efficacy of criminalising coercive control has been contested (Walklate, Fitz-Gibbon, & McCulloch, 2018), building on general challenges to the legal response to domestic abuse – particularly mandatory arrest and pro-prosecution polices (Sherman, 1982). Hanna (2009) has raised concerns that adopting coercive control into law potentially reinforces 'conundrums about women's agency' (p. 1460) and 'complicity in the abuse' (p. 1474). There is a vociferous debate on the merits of introducing coercive control into law (Barlow, Johnson, Walklate, & Humphreys, 2019; Douglas, 2018; Hanna, 2009; Sheehy, 2018; Tolmie, 2017; Walby & Towers, 2018; Walklate & Fitz-Gibbon, 2021) and specific discussions about the legislation in England and Wales (Barlow et al., 2019; Bettinson, 2016b; Bettinson & Bishop, 2015; Bishop, 2016b; Robinson et al., 2017; Walklate et al., 2018).

There has been limited commentary on the likely impact of the Domestic Abuse (Scotland) Act 2018 (Bettinson, 2016b; Burman & Brooks-Hay, 2018; Forbes, 2018; Tolmie, 2017).

The debate highlights the intractable privacy of domestic abuse and the seemingly irreconcilable agency/control dichotomy for victims not willingly engaged in the criminal justice process. The debate about mandatory policies and women's autonomy must acknowledge the state duty to protect individuals from harm, affirmed in the ECHR decision of *Opuz v. Turkey*.[100]

Those against criminalisation argue that: there is no evidence that the legal response 'works'; women are hesitant to engage in the justice process for myriad reasons, yet the law has the power to compel them to attend court and participate (Epstein, 1999; Mills, 1998), and there is scope for abuse to be perpetrated *through* the court process. However, there have also been eloquent proponents (Hanna, 1996), including Coker (2001), who identified a link between women's support for mandatory policies and their interactions with police, underscoring the importance of procedural justice. She observed that, 'victims may experience mandatory policies in ways that affirm their moral worth' (Coker, 2001, p. 857). There is some support for this approach (Buzawa & Buzawa, 2013; for a fuller discussion, see Buzawa, Buzawa, & Stark, 2017), yet such a victim empowerment model presupposes that the interests of the individual victim are primary, focussing on the interests of the *current* victim, not public policies aimed at protecting *future* victims by informing cultural shifts. A gendered framing of the problem assumes that the problem needs to be addressed at a societal level and not just at an individual level. This highlights the tension within feminist literature between affirming victim choice and situating domestic abuse as a gendered, societal problem. Further, it represents an ongoing struggle for feminist academics trying to reconcile agency and victimisation (Dunn & Powell-Williams, 2007; Picart, 2003; Schneider, 2000).

A specific offence of domestic abuse, encompassing coercive control, arguably succeeds in privileging women's accounts[101] and has symbolic importance in recognising and naming abuse. Challenges are undeniable and we should not overstate the 'educative value' of the criminal law (Burton, 2008, p. 68), but criminalisation presents an opportunity to interpret societal attitudes to domestic abuse and better protect those affected. The domestic homicide reviews remind us of the preventability of many intimate partner murders: the legal response is an important part of earlier and more effective intervention in the disruption of coercively controlling behaviour.

CURRENT CHALLENGES

It is too early to know the extent of the impact of the EU (Withdrawal) Act 2018 on the influence of EU jurisprudence. Short term, it shifted focus away from domestic politics and delayed legislation, including the Domestic Abuse Act 2021 in England and Wales. There is potential for the courts to remain influenced by the European Court of Justice and find the judgements persuasive, if not binding.

The Covid-19 global pandemic has impacted everyone in some way. Increased time at home, social distance, job losses, financial uncertainty, digital poverty, and barriers to accessing support have all had a detrimental effect on the prevalence of domestic abuse and have compounded safety concerns for those trying to leave an abusive environment (Shaw, 2020). Support agencies have also faced increasingly testing circumstances as they try to support women remotely whilst juggling their own home life. The lack of collegiate support has been sorely missed and victim advocates report feeling exhausted, not least due to financial uncertainty overshadowing many community projects. The impact of the pandemic on mental health will not be known for many years, but for those experiencing domestic abuse, the challenges have been intensified. Not only has the pandemic helped to drive domestic abuse back behind closed doors, it has also brought the British justice systems to an almost standstill with significant delays.[102] The impact of this further wait for justice is explored in the following chapters.

CONCLUSION

There is cross-party, cross-border commitment to tackling gender-based violence in general and domestic abuse in particular. This is evidenced by consistent policy and strategy in both Westminster and Holyrood. Whilst progress in tackling human trafficking, forced marriage, and female genital mutilation (FGM) has been slower, the determination to deal with domestic abuse is palpable. This topic has cut through traditional boundaries, and the multi-agency response has strengthened the efforts of voluntary and statutory organisations. A concerted national campaign by (Scottish) Women's Aid, *SafeLives* and Refuge, the introduction of IDVAs/IDAAs, and an increasingly effective working relationship between police and prosecutors (Bettinson, 2016a) have also contributed. Nevertheless, policy and legislation are only tools: they need the commitment of those employed to use them. Moreover, reform within the criminal law has not been mirrored in civil procedure where there is arguably greater opportunity to provide remedies and protections (Connelly & Cavanagh, 2007; Walklate & Fitz-Gibbon, 2021); there are certainly greater consequences for women with children. The following chapters explore the ongoing reality of reporting domestic abuse and the barriers to the effective implementation of these laws and policies.

NOTES

1. Available at: Home (coe.int).

2. The Domestic Abuse Act 201 has provisions specifically aimed at meeting the requirements for ratification, including provisions on extra-territorial jurisdiction: see schedule 3, part 1 for England and Wales; and schedule 3, part 2 for Scotland.

3. Available at: https://eur-lex.europa.eu/LexUriServ/LexUriServ.do?uri=OJ:L:2012:315:0057:0073:EN:PDF.

4. This hierarchy is set out by Burton (2008): The Supreme Court Act 1981 governed the High Court and gave power to grant injunctions to spouses and cohabitees, including a power of arrest where there was evidence of violence; the County Court Act 1984 governed the Crown Court and provided similar, but less 'tailored' provision as not specific to domestic violence; and the Domestic Violence and Magistrate's Courts Act 1978 only applied to spouses, giving the court the power to grant orders of protection but no power of arrest unless there was evidence of injury.

5. s2.

6. s3.

7. In civil hearings, the burden of proof is on the 'balance of probabilities', whereas the Crown must prove their case 'beyond reasonable doubt' in a criminal court.

8. s42A.

9. Domestic Violence Crime and Victims Act 2004, s3 amended part IV of the Family Law Act 1996.

10. Domestic Violence Crime and Victims Act 2004, s4 extended the provision to include non-cohabiting couples.

11. Repealed by Sentencing Act 2020, s416. Current provision for restraining orders contained within s359.

12. s31Q relates to civil proceedings; s31R relates to criminal proceedings.

13. Domestic Abuse Act 2021, s63.

14. Domestic Abuse Act 2021, s64.

15. Available at: https://www.justice.gov.uk/courts/procedure-rules/civil/rules/part01/practice-direction-1a-participation-of-vulnerable-parties-or-witnesses.

16. The Civil Justice Council is a non-departmental public body established by the Civil Procedure Act 1997, s6. Its main function is to advise the Lord Chancellor on civil justice and procedure.

17. For a historical overview, see Williams and Walklate (2020).

18. s48.

19. s49; see www.victimscommissioner.org.uk.

20. s49 and s32.

21. s5.

22. s10.

23. Practice Direction (CA (Crim Div): Criminal Proceedings: General Matters) (2013) EWCA Crim 1631; cemented in law by the Criminal Procedure Rules 2015.

24. Vulnerable Witnesses (Criminal Evidence) (Scotland) Act 2019, s5.

25. This is the best case scenario: often, the support person is court-appointed and the witness has never met him/her before.

26. s23.

27. s24.

28. s25.

29. s26.

Law

30. s27 and s28.

31. s29.

32. s30.

33. Previously victims of human trafficking and sexual offences.

34. Domestic Abuse Act 2021, s62 amends s17 of the Youth Justice and Criminal Evidence Act 1999.

35. s76.

36. The concept is based on Evan Stark's (2007) neat encapsulation of the Duluth power and control wheel as 'coercive control'.

37. s76(1).

38. s76(1)(a).

39. s76(2) and 76(6).

40. s76(3)(b).

41. s76(1)(c).

42. s76(4)(a).

43. s76(4)(b).

44. s76(5).

45. s1(1)–(3).

46. s1(4).

47. s70.

48. s71.

49. s68.

50. s4.

51. s22.

52. s57.

53. s65 and s66.

54. s62 and s63.

55. s72–74.

56. s76.

57. s77.

58. s83.

59. s78.

60. See also SWA annual census publications at: www.womensaid.scot – the 2020 Census shows that 51% of women seeking refuge were refused because of lack of provision.

61. s4.

62. Protection from Abuse (Scotland) Act 2006, s32.

63. s8.

64. s11(1).

65. s1 covers the welfare test. For an overview of the application of the 1989 and the provisions in England and Wales, see Black, Bridge, Bond, Reardon and Grewcock (2015) being asked to adjudicate on where children ought to live, the court must take the welfare of the children as paramount and should not make any order unless it is better for the child(ren) than making no order at all.

66. The Children (Scotland) Act 2020, s9 will introduce a register of approved practitioners to conduct welfare reports for court.

67. Inserts s11ZB to the 1995 Act.

68. *LRK v. AG* (2021) SAC (Civ) 1.

69. Inserted by the Family Law (Scotland) Act 2006, s24.

70. s11(7B).

71. The Children (Scotland) Act 2020 amends the 2004 Act to create deemed vulnerable witnesses in some civil proceedings (s5) and prevent those personally involved in a case self-representing, for example, domestic abuse (s4).

72. s19.

73. s20.

74. s21.

75. s22.

76. s23.

77. Freedom of Information (Scotland) Act 2002, s1.

78. Abusive Behaviour and Sexual Harm (Scotland) Act 2016, s2.

79. Criminal Law (Consolidation) (Scotland) Act 2010, s39.

80. s11 inserted s234A to the Criminal Procedure (Scotland) Act 1995.

81. Domestic Abuse (Scotland) Act 2018, schedule 1, part I, chapter 4, 9(1) inserts section 234AZA into the Criminal Procedure (Scotland) Act 1995.

82. Domestic Abuse (Scotland) Act 2018, schedule 1, part I, chapter 4, 8(1) inserts section 210AB into the Criminal Procedure (Scotland) Act 1995.

83. Procurator Fiscal Hamilton against John Donnelly (2021) SAC(Crim)2.

84. 2014 Act, s12.

85. 2014 Act, s9.

86. 2014 Act, s3F.

87. 2014 Act, s28.

88. 2014 Act, s29.

89. 2014 Act, s4.

90. L. Brooks (2018). Available at: https://www.theguardian.com/society/2018/feb/01/scotland-set-to-pass-gold-standard-domesticabuse-law.

91. Includes physical and sexual violence – s2(4)(a).

92. s1(1)(a). s9 creates a presumption as to relationship.

93. The impact of this section on the requirement of corroboration and the definition of domestic abuse is worthy of a separate examination.

94. Schedule 1, chapter 3(8)(2) inserts section into the Criminal Procedure (Scotland) Act 1995.

95. s2(3).

96. s5.

97. s4 (notices) and s8 (orders).

98. Consideration was given to a Victims' Commissioner when drafting the Victims and Witnesses (Scotland) Act 2014, and there was a further parliamentary debate in 2018, but the decision not to introduce the role was defended on the grounds that victims were better served by funding for essential victim services, such as Victim Support. There are advantages to a champion of victims' rights.

99. Walklate, Fitz-Gibbon, and McCulloch (2018).

100. *Opuz v. Turkey Application no. 33401/02, 09/06/09*: a Turkish woman reported her husband to the police for assaulting her and threatening to kill her. The police attended and there was medical evidence of injury. The police progressed the investigation but closed the case when the woman said that she did not want to go to court. Following her murder, the woman's daughter successfully brought a case against the Turkish authorities for failing to protect her mother.

101. Alison Di Rollo, QC, Solicitor General for Scotland, speaking at the Scottish Women's Aid Conference, Edinburgh, 1 December 2017.

102. Statistics for England & Wales. Available at: https://publications.parliament.uk/pa/cm5801/cmselect/cmjust/519/51905.htm; statistics for Scotland. Available at: https://www.scotcourts.gov.uk/official-statistics.

Chapter Three

THE VICTIM EXPERIENCE BEFORE COURT

INTRODUCTION

This chapter begins to tell the story of women's experiences of engaging with criminal justice agencies from an initial call to the police in a moment of crisis until the point that a case may call for trial. It explores themes of agency and trust and the traumatic impact of waiting. In describing women's everyday stresses, the inadequacies of the criminal justice response become apparent: the police response remains incident focussed, while well-intentioned communications tend to be misjudged and mistimed. This chapter explores the impact of criminal justice practitioners focussing on 'punctuation marks' within the process and the impact this has on victims' waiting. While practitioners focus on court dates, reporting targets, and seemingly arbitrary dates to communicate updates, the victim's key dates relate to anniversaries and triggers. This chapter examines how to realign these conflicting timelines to improve communication with victims. Women's accounts are analysed through the lens of significant practitioner experience to relate them back to the process at the macro level (see Bosworth & Kellezi, 2017).

The purpose of this chapter is to:

- Explain the criminal justice process from reporting a crime to the point of trial.
- Tell the stories of women who have experienced the process to highlight barriers to justice.
- Illustrate the barriers to justice for women at the point of reporting.

In the same way that domestic abuse is not all about hitting, justice is not all about the trial. Justice, like the lived experiences of women, is a process: a flawed narrative, punctuated by stutters and hiccups. It is rarely predictable, often dramatic, and always emotional for victims of personal abuse and those professionals seeking to support them (Bosworth & Kellezi, 2017). Women experience a range of responses throughout their interaction with the justice process: resolve, expectation, grief, sadness, confusion, frustration, hope and hopelessness, pride, and disappointment, sometimes all at the same time.

Public awareness and consciousness-raising about the issue of domestic abuse have become the mainstream, and a coherent government approach to ending violence against women and girls continues to develop. Nevertheless, policymakers, together with academics, have focussed on the police and court response, rather than the process before, during, and after these official punctuation marks.

REPORTING TO THE POLICE

Recall from Chapter One, the significant shift in policing approach since the 1970s – across policy and practice. We are far better placed now, but policing of domestic abuse remains inconsistent. An inspectorate report of the police response to domestic abuse in England and Wales found that it 'is a priority on paper but, in the majority of forces, not in practice' and surmised that 'the overall police response to victims of domestic abuse is not good enough' (HMIC, 2014, p. 6). While some officers in every force UK-wide have received training on domestic abuse, more officers respond to domestic abuse calls than have received training. There is also disparity in the level of training from online e-modules to bespoke face-to-face training. Each of the 44 forces across mainland UK have their own governance and approach. In some areas, the response may be dictated by the severity of the offending or the presence of a specialist court and its support infrastructure. While there have been moves across England and Wales to address the recommendations in the HMIC report and there is commitment in Scotland to increased face-to-face training, inconsistencies in approach, training, and prioritisation remain (HMCPSI & HMICFRS, 2020).

It is worth pausing to think about what this means for those who have experienced abuse. For most, reporting a crime and the prospect of going to court is scary. It means formal, sometimes complicated letters in the post. It means waiting for what feels like ages to hear updates, and it may mean giving evidence in court. This can invite further anxiety and, potentially, frustration. Within the context of domestic abuse, these barriers are compounded. The dynamic shifts when the alleged perpetrator of the crime is someone you may have loved and with whom you have had an intimate relationship. If there are children, proving the case may hinge on their evidence. It is no longer just about whether you are strong enough to face the process, it becomes a tough decision to ask your child to give evidence and speak up against a parent.

It is important to appreciate the enormity for women of phoning the police. Yet, for the responding officers, it is also stressful. The volume of reported cases and the emergency nature of many calls mean that domestic abuse is first response policing. The first officer to speak to a victim of domestic abuse may have had some initial awareness training but will not be a specialist. This necessarily places limitations on the initial police response, in terms of the emotional needs and expectations of victims. It is not widely understood that reporting to the police kickstarts a chain reaction of protocols and mandatory policies. Jean, an IDAA, observed:

> *They make a phone call to the police because they're in crisis and distress in their relationship and then, all of a sudden, this whole process starts to roll and it's unstoppable really.*

At this point of crisis, there are emotional, practical, and safety needs. Women need a sensitive and appropriate police investigation from the outset (Brooks & Burman, 2017), but the police are not equipped or resourced to meet all these needs: friction abounds. It takes a police officer between four and six hours to deal with and report a domestic abuse allegation where there are children in the home, but the average police shift is 8–10 hours. These numbers do not add up. It is a tortuous exercise in repeated form filling, multiple reports, and judgement calls. Concurrently, they are applying their basic training on the dynamics of domestic abuse, hopefully providing an empathic response to women and children and fulfilling a specialist role of assessing risk. Meanwhile, a woman has just taken the brave step to report. She is still deciding if she should trust the officer, how much to say and rapidly assessing her own risk.

Women are at increased risk when they attempt to leave an abusive relationship (Monckton-Smith, Williams, & Mullane, 2014; Stark, 2007). Eilidh was aware that there is also heightened risk in reporting:

> *You just terrorise women further, because the belief is, and it's a correctly held belief, he's only going to be angrier because you've reported him. That is correct. He's not going to become, you know, more appeased. It's a risk factor, reporting is a risk factor.*

This risk was not just Eilidh's perception as a victim with fear of reprisals. It was also recognised by Libby in her experience of supporting clients that women are the experts in assessing their own risk:

> *She's the person addressing her safety fears. For all the rest of us who are trying to put things in place for her, it's that woman who is in that position who is the real person who knows what's going to make her safe and it might be that reporting to the police on that day is going to make her more unsafe because that abusive person still has access to her physically.*

Women are making complex safety assessments internally before answering questions. Megan explained why she was not truthful with police officers:

> *They were saying, has he got kids, we need to know for child protection procedures. But that's a whole other realm talking about kids, his ex-partner finding out what he's done to me and I was just*

> *like, he does not see his kids. I lied at that point because I just thought, I can't cope with this, I can't deal with that.*

Thus, it is important that police officers appreciate their responsibility at the point of first disclosure.[1] Women worry they will be neither believed nor heard – summoning up the trust in the police to actually report is a significant hurdle. Hannah explained:

> *The police should recognise, with training, that it's hard for you to talk about it the first time, that it's not a single incident, it's completely different, therefore you can't possibly recall it all the first time, you've never met these people before.*

Phoning the police may be the only point in the process when control rests wholly with the victim although many victims of domestic abuse are subject to third-party reporting and do not even make this initial decision. There is a general expectation of receiving help but no real appreciation of what may follow. As Joyce explained:

> *At that stage, you're trying to tell the whole story, but in a bit of a state. So, having never been through anything like that and only seen it on a television programme … when it actually happens to you, it's mind blowing.*

On being asked how she felt making that initial call and subsequently talking to a police officer, she said:

> *I felt it was all rushed. It was Saturday night, they were busy an' it was just like a domestic type thing. They weren't really listening to me.*

This pinpoints the short period when Joyce felt in control of her situation and highlights the challenges of training front-line officers to deal sensitively with domestic abuse calls at peak times. The outcome of the leap of faith that a phone call represents should not be determined by the timing of the call or the experience or discretion of the officer who responds (Myhill & Johnson, 2016; Westmarland, Johnson, & McGlynn, 2017). Hannah described how reporting to the police was not the opportunity she hoped for:

> *So mentally you have to prepare yourself for when you're ready for that, and I think I was in and out the police station in five hours and I had thirteen years and obviously I know they don't want the full story, they don't want all the ins and outs, but my experience of it, I went in clueless, I had no idea and I believed when I went in there to give my statement that somebody would bring me back at a later point to add to my statement or see if there's anything else you remember.*

Before making such an important decision to share intimate details of love and betrayal, women should understand the process that lies ahead. It is not unreasonable to assume that there will be a further opportunity to add to her statement. It should be a basic service level, rather than an example of best practice. Even where the police response is empathic, the realities of front-line policing can prevent an appropriate response. Megan walked into a police station, by herself, not sure if she was going to report:

> *I was like, I'm just looking for some telephone numbers and the officer said, who's done this to you? And I was crying and he was like, look, I'm going to get a female officer to come and speak to*

you, take a wee seat, so I waited. I waited maybe fifteen minutes, still no-one had come to speak to me, the snow was bad, I knew my mind was starting to play tricks on me, so I just ran.

The officer who spoke to Megan was attuned and recognised some of what had happened to her, but between the initial empathic response and the decision to leave her waiting in a public area of a busy police office on a Saturday night, an opportunity was lost. Megan drove to her friend's house, where she said: 'my friend took it out of my hands', and called the police. She was told that she was at risk of being murdered and urged to report: 'I remember that sticking in my head'. It is difficult to calculate how many others have run from police stations and returned to an abusive relationship. The solution to these barriers ought to lie in advocacy support so that women better understand the process, receive help to safety plan, and have some therapeutic support. However, there is also a need for more honest and detailed guides to reporting and routine scope for statements to be taken over several days, if needed.

ADVOCACY SUPPORT AND RISK ASSESSMENTS

Chapter One explained the role of independent domestic abuse advocates (IDVAs in England and Wales and IDAAs in Scotland), the training programmes offered by *SafeLives* UK-wide, and how risk assessments inform safety planning.

Evidence suggests that an early advocacy intervention complements an empathetic police response (McMillan, 2015). Most domestic abuse models are predicated on local police offering a referral at the stage of reporting. In relation to sexual offences, there have been some efforts to offer support prior to reporting to the police (Brooks & Burman, 2017). The victim advocate was introduced to translate the opaque language of criminal justice organisations, explain the process, safely provide courts with the victim's views, support court attendance, and minimise the impact of secondary victimisation (Burman, 2009; Kelly, Lovett, & Regan, 2005) and other negative impacts on mental health from involvement in the criminal justice process (Elliot, Thomas, & Ogloff, 2014). They are motivated by a will to ensure that women's voices are heard in the court process, but part of their institutional advocacy role involves ensuring that best evidence is secured.

The role of the victim advocate has evolved from its introduction to support specialist domestic abuse courts (Robinson, 2006a). There is evidence to suggest that victims are less likely to retract from the criminal justice process if they are supported by an advocate (Brooks & Burman, 2017; Robinson, 2006a), and advocacy representation lends meaning to the multi-agency risk assessment conference or 'MARAC' (Brooks & Burman, 2017). In both aspects, the strength of the victim advocate lies in his/her capacity to 'privilege the importance of individual experience'. Within the context of uncertainty in which a report is made to the police, this is important.

Advocates seem to understand their responsibility to victims and the balance of emotional and safety needs, as Jean, an IDAA, explained:

> *You realise you are maybe one of the last people to speak to somebody ... when you put down the phone to that person, have you done everything you could in your powers to give them all the information they need and all the options that they've got available.*

The value of such support to provide voice on a woman's behalf and to help navigate the process (Brooks & Burman, 2017; Robinson & Hudson, 2011) was articulated by Laura:

> *I love what ASSIST [advocacy service] did, it's a shame we have to have these things, but see the help they offered. I never had a clue what was happening, I've never been through the court system before, I had no idea ... you were just like a rabbit in the headlights and I think because you were in the middle of this and still trying to recover and still not having a clue what was going on, you weren't very assertive.*

Similarly, the emotional value of such support was summed up by Joyce:

> *A lot of women don't speak up because they don't know about the help that's out there, like ASSIST and how they can actually help, and obviously I know the police have got to put you onto ASSIST, but it's not really recognised. I was petrified and Millie from ASSIST took that, no, she didn't take the full fear away, but she made it easier to go through.*

While this emotionally attuned expertise is invaluable, three interrelated challenges for advocates compromise the level of support. First, despite a consistent training package from *SafeLives*, there is divergence of opinion on the key components of an advocacy model (Blake Stevenson, 2017). For example, some IDVAs/IDAAs believe support must be face to face, whereas others provide a telephone service (Robinson, 2017b). Second, some IDVAs/IDAAs will advocate support for mandatory policies and the benefits of the criminal justice response, whereas others interpret women's agency as incompatible with the uncompromising justice response. Third, advocacy provision is patchy and is not available to all victims.[2] Funding is constrained so services struggle to provide a consistent level of support and must prioritise accordingly. For some grassroots organisations, it means waiting lists and a delay in help becoming available, while for government-funded projects aligned to the court process, it means triage of cases and targeted communications. Approaches vary, but the outcome is the same: women cannot predict what support will be available. Noting that the initial decision to speak to the police may be the only time in the process where women have complete agency, this impact on their informed consent is concerning and presents a compelling case for national advocacy provision to provide a well-publicised, adequately funded, and predictable service.

IDVAs/IDAAs are trained to sensitively assess risk to help women safety plan. Without a national victim advocacy service, these assessments are not applied consistently. The apparent paradox is that the risk assessment is designed to identify and manage high-risk victims, yet victim advocates often assess this to be an inappropriate tool for those most at risk. Professional judgement may override both the decision to carry out the RIC and to revise the RIC score and refer to the MARAC, where there is minimisation and a professional concern. Jean explained: 'if we had a low RIC score, my professional judgement might be that this is scored low because the person is minimising the abuse'. This is consistent with the existing research, which points to IDAA/IDVAs relying on information beyond the risk assessment tool and their own professional judgement (Robinson & Howarth, 2012) and the basic inability of such a tool to deliver 'anything more than a hypothesis' (Walklate & Mythen, 2011, p. 103). As observed by Martha: 'risk is fluid', and Chloe summed up that 'it's an excellent tool, but it's not the be-all-and-end-all'.

POLICE ASSESSING RISK

The risk assessment model has been used by police first responders across the UK since 2009 in England and Wales (DASH[3]) and 2012 in Scotland (DAQ).[4] They are broadly similar and were designed for a more nuanced approach by victim advocates with specialist training and time. However, in isolation, they are a blunt tool. Over 20 questions starting with: 'Are you frightened?' and which go on to examine every intimate aspect of a victim's life. This includes potentially traumatic recall of violence, abuse, and sexual assault, which may never have previously been divulged. It is unsurprising that many women, who have just reported and are speaking to a police officer for the first time, choose not to disclose. If the victim does answer, there remains potential for partial disclosure so that the full extent of offending behaviour and the level of risk are inaccurately assessed. The police invariably conduct a risk assessment before referring the victim to a support agency. This means that the specialist training of IDAA/IDVAs is to sensitively tease out information and the opportunity to conduct an accurate risk assessment is lost. Worse, there is a risk of disengagement when the same questions are asked twice in a short time frame. Translations of numerical scores are unreliable, as different practitioners filter and prioritise different factors (Robinson & Howarth, 2016). Many workers raise concern about police assessing risk. Research shows that the score is consistently lower when a police officer conducts the risk assessment, compared to an IDVA/IDAA asking the same questions (Ariza, Robinson, & Myhill, 2016; Robinson, Pinchevsky, & Guthrie,

2016). Emily voiced this unease about police officers' ability to use the tool appropriately:

> *my concern is that it is not reflected in a risk assessment unless those officers actually decide that it's a risk. And it depends on the officers. But even training does not address that. It's deep-rooted attitudes to what is ok for a man, when the relationship has just ended, it's what your expectation is of his behaviour and if you think it's alright that he's going to harass her. It does not matter what tools you use, that's not going to change how the case is handled.*

For others, including Jean, it was the repetition of asking the same questions within 24 hours:

> *it's like somebody having to repeat their story over and over. They've already told the police this. If we had those answers, we would say 'when you spoke to the police you said this …' It would help if someone said he killed my rabbit that we're not saying, has he ever been cruel to animals? Well, yeah, I told the police that he killed my rabbit. D'you know.*

From a victim's point of view, the same probing, potentially triggering, and possibly insensitive questions are being asked twice, by two different organisations with different purposes. It is therefore unsurprising why women do not feel listened to. This repetitive 'process' is arguably almost as disempowering as not being given an opportunity to speak at all. It is also difficult to persuade victims that a coordinated community response is being adopted for their benefit when this basic information-sharing fails.

What does this mean?

- Women may not call the police, but it is *their* decision to report and tell their story.
- It is a key decision but is imbued with risk, fear, uncertainty, and no real appreciation of the consequences.
- Victims are still considering whether to trust police and how much to disclose.
- There is little appreciation of how complicated it might become to make further disclosures later.
- Assessments of risk and decisions on procedure are often made with partial information.
- The role of victim advocates and support agencies is to listen to women, build trust, help them manage their own safety, and navigate the justice response.
- Research is unequivocal on the benefits of advocacy support.
- Advocacy support tends to come *after* a report to the police.
- The timing of support is misaligned with victim needs.
- The initial risk assessment can be done twice and applying different judgement.
- The effect of repeat questioning can be re-traumatising and trust can be lost.
- Resource constraints lead to advocacy support often being focussed around the key dates in the court process or delayed by a waiting list.

Being overwhelmed by the justice process is a common theme. The value of advocacy in the immediate aftermath is to help demystify the system and provide emotional support. Accepting the benefits of advocacy support is straightforward, but it does not encapsulate the critical or urgent need to be heard, seen, and understood by just one person. There is a growing sense of unmet needs in taking the bold, unchartered step of reporting. The sense of deflation in Laura was visible as she admitted: 'It's exhausting. You're just exhausted in every way'. To be exhausted at the start of the process is isolating and daunting. You need fire and energy to deal with a bureaucratic machine as complex as the criminal justice system. And this is just the beginning.

WAITING FOR COURT

Overwhelmingly, women are expected to wait. They wait for a safe opportunity to report, or worse, until crisis point. While waiting for court resolution, women are waiting for bruises to heal, decisions on housing, referrals for emotional support, reports from schools and bar reporters, contact from his family, civil court resolutions, and (marked) time to pass. The first wait is for the outcome of the initial bail hearing: to know if he has been remanded in custody or if protective conditions of bail have been granted. This is critical to safety planning. Following these initial short, tense waits, women subsequently wait for what can be – and feels like – a very long time to hear if the case is going to court. They wait not knowing how long they are expected to wait, exactly what they are waiting for or if it will be worth the wait. In Chapters One and Two, we explored the consistent rhetoric that has developed to support women to report domestic abuse: civil laws offer women more protection and abuse itself has been criminalised. Yet we remain ill-equipped to fully recognise the cost of reporting and provide meaningful support. Waiting is the main barrier. Waiting *for* court and waiting *at* court are distinct. Waiting *at* court is discussed in Chapter Four.

After the initial adrenalin of reporting, there is further immediate tension: his next move, if the police are taking it seriously, and if there will be a remand in custody or bail conditions. The first calling of the case may be when women are particularly vulnerable, as Megan explained:

> *When he's appeared in court, I knew someone would phone me and tell me what's happened. I was so terrified that I got in my car and drove about with the doors locked and I ended up sitting in a carpark, waiting for the call and I don't think it came until after five o'clock and he was remanded.*

At this point, there is still a nervous energy, a flurry of phone calls and new information to grasp. After this first bail hearing, however, there is a long wait – often months. For some, like Kirsty, activity may feel compulsory to assert some agency, even if the result leads to further frustration:

> *I felt like I kept phoning and asking questions and it always just felt like you were kind of asking too much ... I don't know, I just felt there was so many different people I was phoning and not really getting anywhere ... I felt like the onus was on me to do something, when I'd already done enough to ... I mean, whose job is this? It's not mine. Ehm, does that make sense?*

For others, it can also be a frenetic 'filling of time' and an avoidance of cumulative fears (Forbes, 2010) or as Christine put it: 'Scared to slow down because when I slow down it opens Pandora's Box in my head'. At this stage, women start to experience the insecurity inherent in reporting and the lack of recognition of what it costs to report, which is a further layer of frustration and isolation. Waiting is mundane. Each of us can relate to it on some level so that we assume that it is a necessary aspect of the court process, in the same way that we queue for the supermarket or wait for a train. Yet not all waiting is a banal normality. Some waiting is traumatic: waiting for test results, waiting for news of a loved one, or waiting for court. The global pandemic brought uncertainty and traumatic waiting to many. Unfortunately, it forced further delays to the criminal justice process and tortuous waits and adjournments. Despite the universality of waiting (Foster, 2016; Turnbull, 2016), reactions to and implications of waiting remain personal and subjective. The extent to which women cope with the wait seems to depend on their overall experience of the criminal justice response. For most, therefore, it compounds frustration and feels like an added layer of pressure and anxiety. If there can be one hope, it is that wider experiences of waiting during the pandemic might invite greater empathy and recognition of the traumas of waiting.

THE IMPLICATIONS OF WAITING

Rotter's (2016, p. 97) research on the asylum determination process challenges waiting as passive. She suggests:

> *Even for people who have endured loss, trauma and protracted uncertainty, waiting may, under certain conditions, entail intentionality, action and potential.*

Thus, she attempts to validate the activities of asylum seekers during the determination process and assert their legitimacy within the wait. Armstrong (2015, p. 22) surmises:

'If only we could make waiting [in prison] more useful, it would be more humane'. This is comforting and compelling, but it is difficult to reconcile with the experiences of women who have been the victim of a gendered crime. Any positivity generated during the waiting period is precarious in the shadow of further victimisation (Brooks & Burman, 2017; Burman, 2009; Kelly et al., 2005) where every punctuation mark in the wait is a reminder of trauma. Even where a court diet is not a trigger for the victim, the trigger can be initiated by the perpetrator, as Joyce explained:

> *[…] and then there was wee things, like after any different court cases, like I say, there was umpteen of them, eh, I would maybe start getting loads of curries delivered to my front door.*

Joyce explained her hesitance to report these deliveries to the police and the impact that it had on her:

> *My head was burstin' all the time, I was like, I'm not phoning [the police] I know I'm going to have to go over this big story to talk about curries being delivered, but then it was part of his profile that was to scare me …. But at the time, I didn't look at it like that until the police explained it to me.*

Joyce appears to retain some agency as she chooses not to report the repeated breaches of bail and stalking charges in the curry deliveries after every hearing. Yet, her reason for not reporting discloses a lack of trust in the system. For Joyce, the repeated telling of her story was the trauma, more than the curries on the door: it was not that the curries were delivered, it was that no one recognised the ongoing abuse. Her autonomy was compromised by waiting for two forms of communication. First, 'his' next move: whether he would breach his bail, if she would be safe, and whether he would plead guilty. Second, there is the wait for information from the police, the prosecutor, and support agencies.

Thus, within the layers of waiting – for information, for court, at court, for a result, for the abuse to be recognised and stop – women experience what Foster (2016, p. 14) calls a 'series of nested waits', and their scope for agency remains precarious. So long as women are waiting for resolution of court proceedings, they do not regain control. As explored in the next chapter, this is manipulated by (ex)partners who use the court process to further coercively control her time and movements by enforcing a longer wait. Liz commented that 'I think it's unfair because I'm the victim and he still got to manipulate me when we were going [to court]'. Many participants referenced defence motions to adjourn, which Eilidh recognised can be 'a delaying tactic'.

RETAINING AGENCY DURING THE PROCESS

Victim accounts of the justice process are often muddled. These chaotic narratives reflect a lack of understanding of what's happening, despite involvement in it. After the initial report to the police, comes the reality of being in the mire of multiple court dates dictating the pace of life. If there is a plea of not guilty at the initial bail hearing, the case will adjourn until the ground rules hearing in England and Wales, or the intermediate diet or preliminary hearing in Scotland; thereafter, assuming there has still not been a guilty plea, there ought to be a trial date. Most criminal cases call more than three times: adjournments are common, and cases of domestic abuse are likely to provoke breaches of bail, which result in a fresh process with a new initial bail hearing. Hopefully, the breach of bail is conjoined with the original case and both are prosecuted together, but this leads to further court dates. In cases of domestic abuse, concurrent civil procedure to decide on child welfare is common. Thus, a tentative *I might be brave enough to call the police today and tell them about the abuse* can lead to a convoluted process of repeated court hearings. It is statistically unlikely to lead to a trial and giving evidence in court (Ferguson & McDiarmid, 2014; Green, 2011). Reflecting on the barriers to reporting and the fact that the initial report to the police may be partial – and what is known about serial domestic offending (Robinson, 2017a) – it is not uncommon for further crimes to come to light during the process. Thus, women can be involved in multiple court cases for months, if not years, as the victim of serious allegations of imprisonable offences and party to welfare hearings relating to their own children. It is unsurprising that they emerge at the end of the case(s) unclear on court procedure, the burden of proof, the role of court personnel, and the implications of court decisions for them. Jenn was 'too frightened' to make the initial call to the police. While she was fortunate that the attending officers explained some of the process, it could not prepare her for the reality:

> *and they said, we're going to ask you a question and you need to be relatively sure about how you answer it because how you answer it changes pretty much everything about what happens from this moment on, and they said: this doesn't seem out of the blue, has this happened before? And I knew, I knew that literally when I said yes, it became this thing, it became one of those cases and I became one of those people ... and I was able to say yes, it's happened before ... and that was it: that was the beginning of it all. Fifteen months of chaos.*

Kirsty was aware of her poor understanding of the process and consciously sought information, only sometimes getting the help she was looking for:

> *To get advice, I phoned the Scottish Women's Rights Centre, tonnes! I was trying to find out the system. I went to Victim Support who said they would get back in touch with me and they just never did.*

When she made a complaint about a decision which had been made to exclude further charges, she had no clear understanding of which agency was responsible for making the decision:

> *I didn't understand whether it was the police who wouldn't follow it up or the prosecutor, so I'm not quite sure. I felt like I kept phoning and asking question and it always felt like you were kind of asking too much.*

The implications of feeling like an inconvenience by seeking basic case information are potentially serious. Matilda, a support worker, explained:

> *some women that we work with, they just don't want to put anybody out ... they've always been made to feel like a burden.*

This explains why many women navigate the court process without fully understanding it and without asking for help or an explanation. It also highlights why informed choice is such a critical part of agency. Despite being court-focused support, the IDAA/IDVA model remains choice orientated, as Chloe, an advocacy worker, summarised:

> *My job is not to tell a woman what to do, my job is to suss out what a woman needs and then guide her in her choice but making it plain that it's her choice and empowering her to do something about it with the knowledge of what her choices are.*

Christine provided some insight into the ongoing emotional complexity when she described decorating her house, as part of moving on 'because my house was wrecked with him and smelt of him, so I went mad with the emulsion'. However, she conceded that 'the only room untouched is my bedroom, it's my last taboo; most nights I still don't sleep in it'. Reflecting on this, there is no other crime where such a significant proportion of victims remain living within the locus of such intimate violence, revisiting the trauma every day. This explains the disconnect for criminal justice agencies in identifying appropriate systemic responses to a private dynamic, but Matilda also identifies the ongoing nature of coercive control, beyond the 'end' of the relationship:

> *A lot of women, when they have been abused, they can actually become their own abuser in a way, in their head because they are like ... am I a bad person, and questioning themselves, into believing that. So even though the abuser is out of their life, he's still in their head and they're still saying maybe he was right about that, or maybe he was right about this and so in a way they continue the abuse because they've got it in their head, even though they are out of the actual vicinity physically.*

Matilda explains how this is addressed by support workers:

> *That's why we give a therapeutic service and it's about questioning all the crap that he's put into*

> *their head and that they continue to run around their head.*

It is a challenge to engage and empower women with heavily compromised agency and to give them the opportunity and confidence to ask questions and make informed choices, especially where choices are limited within an adversarial process. Women's Aid's ethos of women-helping-women-helping-women resonates with how some women have shifted from victim to supporter, in their bid to improve agency. For those still experiencing the court process, the role of the advocate is important in building trust and encouraging them to 'question all the crap'. However, it brings organisational responsibility to ensure that confidence in the justice response is warranted and that involvement in the process does not place women at further risk.

CONCLUSION

Regardless of the nature of the abuse, their relationship or their route to reporting, women valued advocacy support as one person to listen to them, believe them, and provide support, as Joyce explained:

> *I was overwhelmed with the support I got. If I didn't have ASSIST and Women's Aid, I wouldn't have had a clue what to do, how to deal with anything. I would have been a lot worse off.*

Nevertheless, women's ability to retain agency and engage in the process is compromised from a very early stage in the process and they quickly feel out of control. Well-meaning, evidence-based risk assessments are diluted in their repetition and breed mistrust. Moreover, as formal and support agencies focus support on the formal punctuation marks in the process, crucial opportunities are missed to dissipate anxiety about the next stage. The impact of this anxious wait influences their engagement with the court process, as we see in Chapter Four.

NOTES

1. This is arguably a responsibility of all potential first disclosure agencies, including social workers, midwives, hospital staff, general practitioners (GPs), and housing officers. For example, see McFeely (2016) on health visitor response.

2. In England and Wales, there was a 26% shortfall in national provision in March 2020 (Domestic abuse victim services, England and Wales – Office for National Statistics (ons.gov.uk)).

3. **Domestic Abuse, Stalking and Honour-based violence** RIC. Further information on the DASH. Available at: www.dashriskchecklist.co.uk.

4. **Domestic Abuse Questionnaire.** The development of a risk model in Scotland is charted in my timeline. Available at: www.glasswallsart.com.

Chapter Four

AT COURT

The weight of expectation described in Chapter Three comes to a climax when a court date looms. This chapter describes seemingly minor frustrations such as uncomfortable chairs and cramped waiting areas before dissecting how this impacts women's already compromised agency. It analyses the disconnect between how women may present at court and the emotional responses they experience within the court building: re-traumatisation from triggers and further waiting, ongoing abuse from an (ex)partner through the formal process, and apparent collusion from criminal justice practitioners.

By the end of this chapter, the reader ought to have gained an appreciation of the extent of institutional gender inequality, by viewing the court experience through the eyes of victims of domestic abuse and the workers who support them. The reader should be persuaded that whilst there are deep-rooted gendered barriers to justice, individual experiences can be improved by small shifts. In short, an argument for procedural justice is developing.

The purpose of this chapter is to:

- Tell the story of women's experiences at court.
- Describe women's attitudes to court outcomes and their impact.
- Show the impact of waiting *at* court and why it is traumatic.
- Illustrate how coercively controlling abuse is ongoing through the process.
- Examine why abuse is possible in plain sight in a seemingly enlightened system.

Chapter Three explored the impact of waiting for a court date, resolution, and an ultimate outcome. This wait for the next thing to happen is distinct from physically waiting in the court building for their case to call, which is explored here. As discussed in Chapter Three, women wait not knowing how long they are expected to wait, exactly what they are waiting for or if it will be worth the wait. Physical responses to court are visceral. Christine was physically sick, Kirsty shut down and was unable to speak within the waiting area, and Sarah admitted that she went straight to the bathroom every time due to acute diarrhoea. The fear of the unknown compounds anxiety surrounding attendance at court, as Sarah explained:

> *I'd never been in a court, I fear courts, I used to go for jury duty and I'd be praying not to be picked.*

Not only do women fear going to court in general terms, their safety fears remain acute. This fear of repercussion comes to a height when they are called to court and may have to face the perpetrator. Jane, an IDAA, pointed out that: 'at that point in time she is more frightened of him'. Christine divulged the sinister reality of where this fear comes from:

> *At the door, he whispered that if he got lifted, he would get me and he'll get me and it does not matter when, if I believe him.*

The criminal courts offer protective measures, and trust in those might offer some reassurance (see Chapter Two). However, this chapter explores some of the barriers to those measures providing meaningful safeguards.

The lack of understanding of the court process adds to the confusion. For Jenn, this presented a challenge:

> *I don't think the passage of time was a bad thing. I mean, it would have been nicer to have had clear parameters and clearer markers, and dates to work up to and a little less kind of, oh well, we've tried, we spent eight hours waiting and it's just not worked out, so can you come back next Wednesday. Because for every day that we were in here, I had spent twenty-four hours, forty-eight hours gearing up for it, then eight hours in here and twelve hours de-briefing and you know, trying to decompress from it afterwards, only to re-emerge into society as a functioning person.*

This encapsulates the link between waiting *for* court and *at* court: it is immediately a confluence of the anticipation and realisation of their fear. Reducing the length of time for a case to come to trial may mitigate distress, but whilst there is a lack of information and a lack of time taken for explanations, any wait will *feel* long.

WAITING AT COURT

This increasingly feels like a pressure pot of emotions. Whilst waiting for court, women have held on. Court personnel assume waiting is an inconvenience and a boring aspect of attending court as a victim. They fail to notice the anxiety experienced by many in waiting. Within the context of overburdened courts, harassed prosecutors, and stretched defence agents, it is likely that victims and witnesses attending court will wait for a long time, and there is no guarantee that 'their' case will call that day. Unfortunately, victims and witnesses are not told this: it is the equivalent of a budget airline telling its passengers to expect double-booking and delays. As a result, there is no management of expectations. Kirsty echoes the frustrations of many:

> *You're sitting there all day with the anticipation and the nerves of, I have to do this and then to be told it's not happening. It's very soul destroying.*

This necessitates repeat visits to court – and longer waiting time:

> *Then you're waiting around and you get told that it's going to be twenty minutes and the prosecutor came to speak to me and he was very pleasant and said, I'll be doing this and this person will be doing this, but you only meet him about well, supposedly twenty minutes before going into court. Twenty minutes turned into three hours and a lunch break and it was that long wait that I found really difficult. I didn't know it was going to take … you know once I was told it was going to be twenty minutes, I was like, ok, I can deal with twenty minutes, but what I couldn't deal with three and a half hours, it was quite difficult.*

Not only was waiting an anxious revisit of trauma and fruition of fears, but Chloe told me:

> *The witness room was really uncomfortable. Those*
> *blue chairs. The first four times I wore my black*
> *dress and my heels, but by the fifth time I thought,*
> *sod it, I'm wearing something comfy.*

Jenn agreed: 'by the third time, I was like, I'm not even buying an outfit for this!' This dwindling respect and growing acceptance does not seem to make the waiting less anxious, nor is a focus on the tangible, physical surroundings surprising. They are dealing with these emotions and reactions at the juncture when they will potentially be called to give evidence, and the prosecution will rely on the quality of that evidence. Within this context, it is unsurprising that these emotional responses impact on their ability to present as credible and reliable witnesses or even to speak up at all. This provides further reason to respond in a more empathic way at earlier stages in the process, which recognises the impact and tension of the wait on individuals and the proceedings. Christine is a trauma nurse within a busy Accident and Emergency Department and has received specialist training to help her dissociate from the trauma to treat the presenting injury. She explains:

> *But what I learned to do, somewhere along the*
> *line, was dissociate from what he was doing when*
> *he was doing it and then what's happened is, I've*
> *probably taken way more shit than anybody else*
> *might have managed to take for such a long time*
> *because I was so good at dissociating.*

Focusing on the discomfort of the chairs and the impracticalities of the waiting room is a way of women dissociating from the trigger of re-traumatisation:

> *When the panic, when the trigger happens, I*
> *dissociate. So, you would look at me and I would*

> *be standing doing the exact same thing, completely frozen, but inside, I'm heaving.*

Thus, women attending court may present similarly to other witnesses but may be simultaneously enduring a complex emotional response (Herman, 2001). Nevertheless, their practical complaints – the noise level, its inappropriateness for children, and the lack of privacy when discussing their case – are valid and far more easily resolved than the internal conflict. Changing the seats is not going to resolve the real issue, but it may lend itself to creating an opportunity where, as Armstrong (2015, p. 20) puts it, waiting becomes more 'humane'.

Eventually, women hear their name being called and are either told that the case has been resolved and they can go home or asked to go into a courtroom to give evidence. It feels like a game of chance.

Being Sent Home

Laura's daughter was cited to give evidence at the trial against her father. After waiting, she was not called as he pled guilty. She explained her daughter's emotional struggle:

> *She said, so that's it? I don't get to tell my story. And I said, no. And she said, because I think somebody, and this is what she said, I think somebody needs to know just how bad he is and then maybe, because it's my dad and I do love him, but I don't want to see him.*

The feeling of unanswered questions, lack of resolution, and ongoing safety fears resonated with those whose case did not proceed to trial and who did not get the opportunity to speak. Ayesha felt so ignored after the conclusion of the case against her ex-husband that she 'cried and I'm kind of helpless and I kind of begged, but I was told, that's it, it's done. Now live with it'. Hannah told me: 'I know why the prosecutor didn't phone me back, after what had happened, it would have been hard to phone me'. For both Ayesha and Hannah, not only was their emotional need unmet by simply taking time to provide them with an explanation, the failure to respond to them arguably compounded their trauma. Thus, it is not only in the courtroom but also in the wider justice process that an empathic response is important.

Ayesha's parents and wider family all live in Pakistan, and her only family in Scotland is her sister and family. Amidst the compound barriers of language and culture (for a discussion of intersectional victimisation, see Westmarland, 2015), she waited at court on her own; with her young children; and, on occasion, with her niece revising for a school exam. A brief visit to any court waiting room would show its unsuitability for young children or learning. Ayesha describes waiting all day to be told that an interpreter had not been organised:

> *One time my case came back after all day waiting and they didn't even phone, my interpreter wasn't there and one of the prosecutors, she goes, ehm, let's go without him. No, I've been waiting for this case and right last moment if you were told your interpreter is not there, you're just going, you want every bit to be right and I was so panic, I was so nervous and crying, I would feel more comfortable because there's a lot of vocabulary there, there's a lot of words I don't understand and I want to say everything and just speaking my way.*

Tears of fear and frustration are understandable, yet Ayesha would have presented to busy court staff as hysterical and unpredictable. The inadequate response was, presumably, due to a busy prosecutor with a lack of understanding of the consequences for Ayesha. She was fortunate to have the support of an IDAA who contacted the prosecution office before each subsequent hearing to ensure witnesses had been cited, an interpreter had been ordered and screens would be in place. Ayesha initially reported long-term coercively controlling domestic abuse and marital rape, which must have taken inordinate bravery: 'in my culture, in our society, we don't even use that word'. During the criminal case adjournments and civil child welfare hearings, Ayesha reported harassment within the civil courtroom and numerous breaches of bail. The case had become more complex:

> *So I've been giving big statement to the prosecutor, after a year my statement was this size* [illustrates with hands the size of a couple of paragraphs]. *Let's cut this or that was not charged, so every time when I was going to the court, one thing was going away, so when after a year my case was deserted, is that the word, it was only one charge left ... Sheriff felt this case was going on too long and it's nothing. Why was nothing?*

To find the strength to speak up, the courage to endure, and the agency to assert that her voice needed an interpreter but ultimately feel disbelieved is re-traumatising and has left Ayesha feeling 'kind of helpless' with recurring nightmares and ongoing anxiety. Hannah encapsulated the reality of these feelings and the impact of unanswered questions:

> *You can't just phone up the judge and be like: what's the script, why did you do that? And I think that is a powerless thing and to have that on the back of this kind of case is quite hard.*

The basic requirement for an explanation and to understand the process is reasonable. For some, after the repeated adjournments, there is a trial, and the moment comes when their name is called to go into the courtroom and give evidence.

Giving Evidence

It is important to pause at this point and imagine who is going into court to give evidence. Domestic abuse inevitably invokes the old adage of *Why doesn't she just leave?* Epstein (1999, p. 78) describes this as a rhetoric which 'assumes a false black-and-white model of human relationships'. This is also reflected in a broader societal view of the perpetrator. There have been some attempts to challenge fixed identities within the criminal justice process (Garland, 2001). However, in the domestic abuse trial, the fiction of a 'halo' victim and 'devil' accused endures (Simon, 2007, p. 77). Such a cast list invites a 'remote' prosecutor and a 'tyrannical' judge, thus compromising the accused's procedural rights (Crawford & Goodey, 2000; Hoyano, 2015) and reinforcing impediments to an emotionally intuitive justice response. It also raises the bar on the expectation of an 'ideal victim' (Christie, 1986). There is a systemic failure to recognise the complexity of private intimate relationships within publicly recognised criminality. It is within the context of this layered response of preconceived ideas and the weight of expectation of how a victim should present, that women hear their name called.

Court culture remains unfavourable towards objections to cross-examination (Zydervelt, Zajac, Kaladelfos, & Westera, 2016) despite recent jurisprudence.[1] Evidence which ought to be deemed inadmissible on the grounds of irrelevance is often admitted, and it is unsurprising that adverse conclusions are drawn about victims' credibility. In the context of being badgered, cajoled and painted badly, reluctance and hesitance to attend court, and give evidence are understandable. As Jenn admitted: 'I felt so small'. Moreover, withdrawal from the process may seem like the only way of re-asserting individual control when they feel such pressure, and no one interjects to protect them. Kirsty gave an example:

> *And the questions he asked. They make a big long statement you don't agree with and then they throw in a question that the answer to is yes, you're kind of like, the answer is yes but I don't agree with the statement that you've said and I felt that I had to be on the ball.*

Eilidh had a particularly gruelling experience:

> *It was probably closest to one of the worst experiences I've ever had in my life. I can't imagine how (my child) feels because it was horrific. You stand for too long, physically, but every time I sat down they couldn't hear me, so I had to stand back up. I was called a liar for three and a half hours and nobody objected.*

Sadly, she observed:

> *And it was allowed, it was encouraged in fact by the prosecutor's silence ... because had he objected, I don't think it would have been allowed.*

Liz also had a negative experience:

> *In the criminal trial I got told I was very manipulative. You always get your own way don't you? I was like: Pardon?! I'm the victim! Not him! And it was like, really nasty, you know, you're lying*

> *aren't you? And nobody objected to anything his lawyers were saying. I was the bad person.*

This was compounded by the lack of professionalism of the defence agent afterwards:

> *My sister hadn't given evidence yet and she was in the waiting room, and his lawyer came into the witness room on his phone and said, yeh, just had her on the stand and I've just ripped her to pieces. And it was me he was talking about.*

It is on the day of the trial that feelings of being unheard and disbelieved feel most acute. Unless there is a conviction, Ayesha's words echo, and there is little prospect of victims feeling believed. A plea of guilty ought to be positive, but if a lesser charge is negotiated (Baldwin & McConville, 1981; Sanders & Jones, 2011) and aspects of the allegation deleted, without explanation, this can also feel like a sign of being disbelieved, if the rationale for the decision is not explained. Laura sums this up:

> *Surely somebody's lies can't be more convincing than your truth? So he can stand there and say whatever he likes but our stories are all pretty much the same, what happened happened. We're not adding anything, we're not taking anything away, what happened happened. But I think the basic premise must be the same for everyone, your voice just is not heard. And there is a huge lack of understanding about the effect that this has.*

Barbara echoes this sentiment:

> *As if my word isn't enough. As if, that if it went up to court, my word against his, my word isn't actually enough for what he did over the years.*

Elaine felt keenly that the court did not understand the impact of historic abuse or the dynamic of coercive control:

> *It is hard when you're talking about feelings because you can't prove that somebody's a liar. He's great at lying and I just tie myself up in knots and it would be good if the court could see that.*

For Eilidh, it was the impact of her young child, assaulted by his father, not feeling believed:

> *And he's disillusioned. He just thinks – sighs – what's the point? What's the world mum? The world is full of liars. Look what's happened to us: we told the truth and we've suffered.*

These negative experiences are not encountered as a one-off. Having a day in court is a misnomer. In reality, there are multiple proceedings, compounded by adjournments, running in a confusing mesh.

THE IMPACT OF CONCURRENT CIVIL PROCEEDINGS

For those victims of domestic abuse who are also mothers, their focus tends to be on the civil process as their main priority is the safety of their children. Women understand that there are two processes running in parallel: the civil procedure that will decide on the welfare of their children and the extent of parental responsibilities and the criminal court that will decide if the domestic abuse privately experienced is publicly recognised as a crime. Yet, by the end of those processes, they will make little – if any – distinction and are likely to reflect holistically on their experience of court (Burton, 2008; Cook, Burton, Robinson, & Vallely, 2004; Robinson,

2007). The practical effect for them is repeated, disheartening attendances at court. Against this backdrop, it is frustrating that many of the protective special measures available in the criminal court are not available in the civil court. There is little awareness of the limited availability of special measures in civil procedure. There is no funded court advocacy programme, IDVAs or IDAAs, for the civil court. During civil procedure, women share a waiting room with their ex-partner and his family; sit opposite him, across a small table in the courtroom; and are approached by him on the way in and out of the court building. Ayesha told me: 'I was waiting there and his body language was very aggressive'. Liz explained that: 'he could sit right beside me for my child welfare hearing, I couldn't do anything about it'. If bail conditions are in place from the criminal court that the accused should not approach or contact the complainer/complainant, then such approaches within the corridors of the court building are brazen. However, there is little faith in the reassurances that breaches of bail imposed by the criminal court will lead to arrest, as Joyce rationalised:

> *Court was very very frightening. I still felt unsafe, even though I was in a safe room. He breached the bail conditions a few times and he never got put away.*

Not only is this distressing for women and undermines the value of the support available in the criminal court, it can contradict a court order. Women referenced bail conditions being in place from the criminal court that her ex-partner was not allowed to approach or contact her in any way, but she was required to attend the civil court hearing, wait outside the courtroom beside him, and sit across the table from him.

As Liz explains:

> *I had already had to face him taking my child to contact and I had no protection in the contact, so what was the point in putting a screen up?*

Ayesha echoed this:

> *Once I've got screens, not to face him and then civil court, when I go, he's sitting right in front of me. Does that make any difference? I goes, I don't want to, he would move, I know what he does, he would cough and he would make the kind of movements that's my heartbeat is going fast because I don't want to face that person, I've lived enough and I don't want to see his face – and you are giving screen protection so I don't have to see him in another court and then I go regarding my daughter's child welfare hearing and I'm sitting right in front of him. (pause) And he's on bail condition.*

For women experiencing both procedures concurrently, meaningful protection in the criminal court is rendered meaningless. The limitations on the availability of protective measures in the civil court are explored in Chapter Two. Unlike the criminal court, where there is only a requirement to attend court in the event of a trial, parties to civil proceedings attend hearings from the outset in the hope that matters resolve without the need for a proof. Recall that protective measures can only be sought at proof. Thus we have a state response to one aspect of a problem that quickly becomes ineffectual – despite best intentions – because of a limited, narrow consideration of the issue. Policy considerations have been around the protection of vulnerable victims and witnesses in the criminal court when they ought to have considered that victims of domestic abuse are often mothers, that domestic abuse often brings separation of a parent and child, and that there will be an overlap between the civil and criminal procedure. The special measures afforded in the criminal court lose their meaning and protective qualities if they fail to protect the same women coming to the same court building on a different day. The impact of being promised protective measures and advocacy support that is effectively selective is that women feel understandably confused. Instead of a clear message, they hear assertions, followed by caveats, followed by an awkward silence.

ONGOING COERCIVE CONTROL THROUGHOUT THE COURT PROCESS

Despite promises of a gendered understanding of domestic abuse, robust policies to criminalise abuse and a concerted multi-agency effort to support those reporting, we have seen many flaws in the process. Compounding all barriers, the greatest challenge remains new and unforeseen abuse, in plain sight of the criminal justice agencies.

It is inevitable that where there is acrimony between two parties to a court dispute, that one party might seek to manipulate the process by seeking spurious adjournments or instructing a solicitor to make a moot point. These are usually recognised by the judge for what they are and disallowed. Yet some domestic abuse perpetrators seem capable of sinister and coercive means to attempt to maintain control. Joyce told me what happened to her the day after a court hearing:

> *I got up for work at half past four and let my wee dog out and all my ropes* [washing line] *had been*

> *cut and I was frightened he was behind the shed and I noticed, I've got two special gnomes, one was my gran's and the other one my late dad had bought me and he knew that and they were gone.*

Chapter Three recorded the impact on Joyce of receiving numerous curry deliveries to her house after each court hearing: something and nothing. She also reported seemingly minor breaches of bail, where her ex-partner was near her place of work. When we know that she starts work so early in the morning; when we know that the curry deliveries were made by hacking into her broadband account to access her payment details and her new address; when we know that her ex-partner also bought her a gnome when they were still together and that he had placed it in between her two special ones we understand this pattern of abusive and intimidating behaviour, much of which may seem relatively minor in isolation but accumulates to a significant safety risk. This is alarming when she has taken the step of reporting to the police and presumes that this generates a level of openness, monitoring, and safety.

The criminal justice process intended to help them was also used as a tool by the perpetrator for further abuse. The range included delay tactics through repeated motions to adjourn, coughing, verbal and non-verbal cues within the courtroom, approaches in the corridor, messages sent through children, and deploying the mandatory arrest policy to secure the arrest of the victim as a perpetrator. Julie called the police at 4 a.m. because her partner assaulted her in front of her son and was threatening to kill her. Following a previous call, there was already a police vulnerability marker on her phone:

> *He came up to my bedroom with a knife and I ended up going for the knife and I stabbed him because he'd been threatening to slit my throat if*

> *I phoned the police again and I was still waiting another ten minutes before the police came and I got charged with attempt murder.*

Despite several efforts to report to the police, Julie found herself in the situation of defending herself, convinced that she and her son were about to be killed. The mandatory arrest policy[2] led to Julie and her son both being arrested, which forced her to make an admission to secure the release of her son and resulted in a prosecution against her, which, after protracted investigation, was discontinued after a year and resulted in the loss of her tenancy.

Sarah was reported several times to the police, leading to her feeling a constant need to justify her actions over the smallest things and a paranoia that she may have done something wrong. One evening, two officers attended her home in relation to an allegation that she locked her front door at night. When she challenged the sergeant the following day, his response was symptomatic of someone who potentially recognised ongoing control by the perpetrator but chose not to challenge it. She described her interaction with the sergeant:

> *I am here because you sent two officers to my door. Oh yes, I know I did. We had your ex-partner in and I felt he was taping me, he had his mobile phone up his jacket sleeve and it was just easier to say we'd investigate.*

Liz described a similar experience:

> *His now wife used to send the police to my door every other week accusing me of something to try and make me look like a bad person. They never charged me with anything. He made up some amount of random lies.*

Research has warned of an increase in wrongful arrests of victims, as a result of mandatory policies (Brooks & Kyle, 2015), and some liberal feminists have suggested that, as with presumptions in favour of prosecution, they limit women's agency and thwart equality (Nichols, 2014). This is to misconstrue the issue. The presumptions in favour of action are amongst the only policies which seek to address gender inequality. They are a recognition that women are at risk of further manipulation and coercively controlling behaviour. So long as women have the power to 'choose' whether a prosecution proceeds, perpetrators will have the power to evade justice by forcing an end to proceedings. Presumptions in favour of arrest and prosecution are not blanket erasers of professional discretion. However, it relies on officers recognising coercively controlling behaviour, which is predicated on adequate training in the dynamics of abuse (Barlow, Johnson, & Walklate, 2018; Myhill & Hohl, 2016; Robinson et al., 2012). Recalling the current lack of face-to-face training narrated in Chapters One and Three, this explains the anecdotal evidence in the current data relating to an increase in dual arrests which is borne out by other academic literature (Brooks & Kyle, 2015).

This highlights the need for quality training and illustrates the inaccuracy of the public/private dichotomy. In the same way that domestic abuse is more than physical assaults and includes psychological and emotional abuse (Westmarland, 2015), so the 'violence of privacy' (Schneider, 2000) is not simply behind closed doors, but infiltrates the relationship beyond the home and influences wider perceptions of the victim. The fact that the abuse can continue within the courtroom, the child contact centre, lawyers' offices, and police stations means that women's narratives have not yet been fully understood, and gender inequality remains within structural responses. It is symptomatic of wider societal misunderstanding. Great strides have been taken since women first marched to *Reclaim the Night*[3] and scratched around a flee-ridden building in West London to provide the first refuge places (Pizzey, 1974). Yet, whilst legislation to criminalise psychological and financial abuse, improved training programmes, legislation to protect victims and witnesses, and policy developments are all welcome, there is still a lack of understanding of what it means to report intimate partner abuse.

This explains why ongoing coercive control is possible, apparently in the open, even during the court process. Kirsty described getting letters for her 20-month-old baby ahead of court dates, despite bail conditions. For Liz, it felt like her ex-partner had control throughout the whole civil and criminal court processes:

> *See if he had taken me into a corner and beaten the living daylights out of me, I would have got over it. Alright, it would have taken a wee bit of time, but I would have got over it. See the mental damage that somebody does to you, you never get over it. The mental damage is forever lasting and the system does not help when they fight against you and they don't believe you. He had so much control over me at every point. Nobody objected or stopped him.*

She provided an example of taking her daughter to a child contact centre and asking her afterwards how she got on:

> *I can't tell you, it's a secret. Why can't you tell me? It's a secret, daddy told me not to tell you anything. And that was the start of it ... and all her problems started to get really bad and she didn't want to go to school.*

Through Liz's perseverance over four years, this ongoing control was eventually recognised by the civil court, when the evidence of a child psychologist was admitted 'to say Ada was being mentally abused by her father and contact got stopped'.

The slow response by the court and the need for expert evidence to persuade the sheriff are perhaps less surprising when considered within this context of the wider community, where the challenge of acknowledging abuse was highlighted by Laura:

> *Even when people recognise what's happening, it's such a difficult one to broach. How do you say to somebody, I think he's being horrible to you, I think this is what's happening?*

Translating this to the courtroom, Eilidh questioned whether professional training was sufficient and challenged the efficacy of expecting police and prosecutors to deal with cases of domestic abuse appropriately, as part of general duties:

> *There are a lot of people who don't get domestics, if you don't have that background and you don't have an insight in any way, they're really hard on [victims].*

Despite this nuanced understanding of the complexity of their own situation and empathy for the difficulties faced by others to recognise it and respond appropriately, women attempt a dignified response. However, when a catalogue of abusive action is permitted, ignored, or unrecognised within the justice process, an emotional response is unsurprising and explains why women ultimately feel unheard.

CONCLUSION

The cumulative effect of the wait for and at court reignites feelings of powerlessness and a lack of autonomy – that someone else retains control – and is reflected in their disengagement from proceedings and frustration. There was an overwhelming sentiment that criminal and civil justice practitioners failed to take the time to listen to them and consequently that their time 'spent' waiting was devalued (Rotter, 2016, p. 88).

What leads to these women collectively feeling disbelieved? Would they feel so disillusioned if they had not had the emotional build-up of a protracted and uncertain wait? Would they be able to rationalise the court outcome better if the process had been clearly explained? Courtroom dramas show pithy ripostes between good-looking, sharply dressed lawyers, a victim with a compelling story, and there is always justice in the end. In contrast, a picture emerges of years of silence punctuated by a disclosure to the police that sets in motion a well-meaning but inadequate response that is defined by months of waiting in the dark; waiting at the point when there was a call for help; unanswered questions; criminal charges that do not reflect the complexity of an abusive relationship; a prosecutor who is untrained to deal with the emotions of a frayed victim; and the challenge of proving intensely private, highly manipulative behaviour to a criminal standard of proof. The court relies on rules of procedure, behavioural protocols, and centuries of tradition for public prosecution of societal wrongs: it is not designed to stop and hear the voices of women. The next chapter examines women's reflections of the court process and sentence and whether, ultimately, it was *worth it*.

NOTES

1. *Robert Spinks* v. *Procurator Fiscal, Kirkcaldy* (2018) HCJAC 37; *Duncan William Begg or Dreghorn* v. *HMA* (2015) HCJAC 69 applied the jurisprudence from England and Wales: *R* v. *Lubemba* (2015) 1 WLR 1579; *R* v. *Jonas* (2015) EWCA Crim 562.

2. There is guidance in both jurisdictions on identifying the primary perpetrator so this should not have happened. England and Wales: Domestic Abuse Guidelines for Prosecutors|The Crown Prosecution Service (cps.gov.uk); Scotland: Revised joint protocol on domestic abuse (copfs.gov.uk)

3. Began in 1977 and remains pertinent in 2021: visit Reclaim the Night: Home.

Chapter Five

AFTER COURT

For victims, perceptions of justice are described as 'kaleidoscopic' (McGlynn, Westmarland, & Downes, 2017). For some, an NHO or restraining order is a relief; for others, it is not enough. Sentencing will only be meaningful and perceived positively when it is contextualised by an understanding of the process. For most, emotional responses to court and feelings surrounding the case are not driven by the outcome but by the process.

The preceding chapters explored the impact of waiting *for* and *at* court. This chapter explores the aftermath and impact of final disposals.

The purpose of this chapter is to:

- complete the *whole* story of women's experiences of reporting domestic abuse and the court process;

- demonstrate the importance of timely and accurate information (particularly around sentencing) and managed expectations; and

- summarise potential sentencing outcomes within the context of how they may be experienced.

POSSIBLE OUTCOMES

For some, the conclusion of one case is only the end of a chapter. They will be re-victimised and asked to go through the whole process again. If they are in a new relationship and the perpetrator is different, myths and preconceived judgements will call her credibility into question. If she has returned to a known abuser, judgements will be harsh. Even where there is not a further criminal prosecution, there may be ongoing civil proceedings. For others, the wait continues for the outcome of a sentence because there has been a plea or a finding of guilt. In these circumstances, a range of sentences is available, including imprisonment or a community-based disposal, which involve a deferral of sentence[1] for background reports on the accused/defendant. Community-based disposals vary, but include perpetrator programmes[2] as part of a constructive deferred sentence and ongoing monitoring by the judge,[3] magistrate,[4] or sheriff.[5] For high-tariff or serial offenders, research suggests good outcomes from targeted perpetrator programmes (Phillips, Kelly, & Westmarland, 2013; Robinson, 2006b; Robinson & Clancy, 2015, 2020).

More generally, social work reports may also suggest electronic monitoring which increases victims' sense of safety (Arenas, 2017; Erez & Ibarra, 2007) and is considerably cheaper than imprisonment although there is often frustration that it is a soft option (Graham & McIvor, 2015).

The increased use of NHOs in Scotland and restraining orders in England and Wales aim to allay safety fears where the level of offending proved does not merit a more punitive sentence. In effect, it extends bail conditions beyond the life of the case. In England and Wales, The Domestic Abuse Act 2021 provides for Domestic Abuse Protection Orders that go further than preventing a person from approaching an individual or address and can impose duties to comply with behaviour, including electronic monitoring.[6] In Scotland, the sheriff has a duty to consider an NHO in the event of conviction.[7] Such orders aim to reassure victims' safety fears through ongoing protection, but the time-limited nature has been called into question.

A financial penalty is competent, although it is arguably not appropriate as it may perpetuate financial abuse if there is an ongoing relationship or there are dependent children. None of the women in this research experienced the court granting a fine. However, some did experience an admonition.

In England and Wales, it is open to the judge to give the offender an absolute discharge or a conditional discharge. An absolute discharge means that the offender will have a criminal record of the conviction, but no sentence is imposed.[8] A conditional discharge is similar but carries consequences for re-offending: if the offender is convicted of an analogous offence, the court can sentence on both offences.

In Scotland, there is no conditional discharge. An offender can be given an absolute discharge or admonished. An absolute discharge is rare: the offender will have a criminal record of the conviction, but the conviction will be automatically 'spent' for disclosure purposes. An admonition means that there is a disclosable record of the conviction, but no sentence is imposed.[9]

Each of these outcomes presupposes that there has been a prosecution. Perhaps the most challenging outcome of all is a false start; a case that does not proceed from the outset because of insufficient evidence.

Despite this choice of disposals available, the women in the present research experienced a limited range of outcomes. Their responses of despondency, confusion, hurt, anger, and (further) exhaustion lead them to believe that it may not have been worth it. The women who expressed positive views of the outcome believed that by reporting they were helping other women, not that the process had helped them as individuals. Whilst their narratives in Chapters Three and Four affirmed the value of advocacy support, its limitations become clear when reading the end of the story and a case emerges for consistent multi-agency responses at an earlier stage. IDVAs/IDAAs should augment support for women, as they are not a panacea to offset the limitations of the response of other agencies.

NO SENTENCE: FEELING UNHEARD

It takes courage to report, and we have seen in Chapter Three that women are often more at risk when they report (Monckton-Smith, Williams, & Mullane, 2014; Stark, 2007). Janie, an advocacy worker, explains the impact where there is no prosecution:

> *It may be that she's phoned the police before, they've arrested him, she's spoken to the police, it's gone to court and perhaps there's not been enough evidence and he's walked back out. He's been liberated. So, that reinforces to her that nothing's going to happen. She's not got the understanding of the evidence that's required for a case to proceed through court and someone be prosecuted. All she knows is that she's been hit again, it's been violent, she's called the police and it's not gone anywhere. She feels that it's reinforcing what he tells her that nobody'll believe you, nobody'll say anything, nobody'll believe that this is going on. So that can sometimes make women step back as well.*

The case may come to an early, abrupt finish if there is insufficient evidence, but it may also stutter if women themselves are unable to engage. Labelling them 'reluctant' is unhelpful and fuels the rhetoric that they 'should just leave' (Epstein, 1999). Instead, there should be greater understanding of the continuum of domestic abuse (Kelly, 1987) and a nudge towards prosecution in a wider context. Janie describes what might be best understood as prosecuting for tomorrow:

> *I suppose you're also trying to help the prosecutor and say, look, this isn't just about today about her being questioned in court, this is the dynamics of abuse, this is what can sometimes happen and as much as we want a prosecution here and as much as we want a woman who's going to give evidence, it's not that she doesn't want to talk to you, it's just that she can't. At this point in time, she can't and based on how the prosecutor deals with that woman can have a big impact on further reporting and coming back to court.*

Janie underscores the disconnect between being labelled unwilling whilst being unable and the impact that may have on a victim's future safety if they lack confidence in the justice process. Victims will only be safe when they have the confidence to come forward again.

THE IMMEDIATE AFTERMATH: AN ANTI-CLIMAX AND THE REALISATION OF FEARS

The building pressure point of emotions described in Chapters Three and Four culminates in the end of the criminal justice response. Having occupied a great deal of women's emotional investment over a period of months or years, the end point can be abrupt. The way the whole case culminates in the ultimate outcome is described by Emily:

> *It's horrific. I've sat for days with witnesses and they're absolutely terrified. To have to go through that time and again is absolutely horrific … in the situation where women are physically shaking, they're frightened to go for lunch, they don't want to bump into him. And I think if you get a good outcome, it helps to make it all worthwhile, but if the case falls, it's devastating and I think in some ways it furthers the abuse, it's almost like the system perpetuates the abuse and it reinforces the fact that women aren't taken seriously and he can do whatever he likes.*

In response to being asked what a good outcome looks like, she observed:

> *I suppose it's different for different people. If she's got confidence in the prosecutor, it makes such a difference because it's about putting yourself in the hands of someone that she trusts. That's a luxury women don't have when they're going through.*

Christine sums up the false expectations:

> *That's the way it leaves you feeling, like your story's untold. And at no point at the start of it, did I feel the need to tell my story. But by the time court came, I had psyched myself up that that's what was going to happen and then we would all be ok after that. That's kind of what, you know, we'll go to court, we'll tell the truth, he'll get a proper jail sentence and we'll all feel like justice has been done.*

Christine's expectations were shaped by her involvement in the process. It seems easy to dismiss hopes of a trial, truth-telling, and just outcomes, as misapprehensions of how the process really works. Yet, Christine's experience suggests that the criminal justice and third-sector agencies bear some responsibility for her expectations. None of these women were motivated to phone the police in a search for justice. They called – or a call was made on their behalf – in a moment of crisis. Their subsequent engagement with agencies led them to believe that there would be a trial, at which they would give evidence. For some, there was hope of a plea. Their fear and nervousness around this process, manifested in a description of being sick on the court steps, is dissipated by galvanising the little agency they have. As they have limited understanding or control over the process, their ability to tell the truth and be heard is a fixed anchor.

It seems that organisations emphasise one potential version of events as an ideal, where women expect that they will give evidence at a trial and, subsequently, that their voice will be heard, and 'justice' will be done. Cast in this light, the need for accurate and realistic information provision becomes an imperative if criminal justice agencies are not to bear some responsibility for causing further trauma. There may be a perception/reality gap for victims, but it seems that the expectation of an ideal is perpetuated by the agencies that understand the process but sometimes fail to disclose the range of possibilities. It is thus unsurprising that women report confusion and lack of understanding around the outcome of 'their' case.

The next section focuses on examples through the eyes of different women and how they reconciled sentence. The aim here is not to critique available sentencing options but to focus on the impact of court outcomes for victims of abuse.[10]

ANSWERING WHYS?

Laura asked a simple question: 'But why can't I be believed?'

There are two ways in which information is important to victims after trial: safety advice and explanations for decisions. Both are important for long-term acceptance and understanding to prevent Laura's sentiment of not being believed. Jenn's ex-partner was sentenced to a period of imprisonment, against which he appealed. Jenn describes walking freely around town for the first time in months, safe in the belief that he was in prison. One day, she received two voicemails, which gave conflicting information. When she could speak to someone, she was told that her ex-partner had been released from prison:

> *He's been released. And I was like: OK. When? Last week! And I was like, what?! I didn't know … suddenly there was this weird acknowledgement that he could have been anywhere, for days!*

Beyond this need for basic information upon which to safety plan, there is also a need to understand the outcome and decision-making of the court process. Provision of information is an aspect of the process that has been addressed, but could be improved (HMIC, 2014; L. Thomson, 2017), and within which best practice requires little additional effort from practitioners and no legislative or policy change.[11] It is thus frustrating that women continue to report a lack of explanation or reasons for decision-making. Moreover, this often reflects a lack of understanding of what is possible within the confines of the adversarial system. Practitioners do not always manage expectations, despite policy-level commitments to provide reasons. Barbara told me:

> *There was no explanation for why it was brought to lesser charges or why it went off and we didn't have to give evidence. There's still a big question mark, I don't know why.*

Ayesha, whose story we heard in Chapter Four, was raped by her husband, placed under inordinate community pressure, and asked at court to give evidence without an interpreter when an administrative oversight meant one had not been ordered, explained:

> *I need to live all my life with this now. I've been given no justice. I've been told I'm right, we believe you, but outcome didn't say they believe me. I think so nobody believed me. If they believed me, they would have given me justice. It was no easy for me to talk about what happened, to everything ... the word I've used that I don't even use that word in my community, I only had that courage because I knew it was the truth ... they didn't have an explanation. But why? They didn't have an answer to my whys.*

This testimony highlights the gaps in current training and understanding, despite organisational and institutional commitment to improve. The rhetoric and the reality remain misaligned.

THAT'S NOT WHAT HAPPENED: WHEN THE SENTENCE DOES NOT REFLECT LIVED EXPERIENCE

Christine did not call the police. Initially, she admitted that her ex-partner had threatened to kill her and her daughters by setting fire to their house. Eventually, she told them about the bruises and, much later, she disclosed sexual abuse. Prior to the trial, the prosecutor spoke to her and told her that a plea had been offered. It is clear from the other women's stories that this does not always happen. The decision by the prosecutor on whether to accept a partial plea is made in the public interest: the interests of the victim are only one aspect of that. Nevertheless, the victim interest is a compelling aspect of the decision-making process and consulting Christine reflects good practice. The sexual abuse was hidden from her young children and she learned on the morning of the trial that, despite the court being closed, there would be a court reporter. Endorsing the plea felt like her only option but inevitably led to the sentence being for lesser offending. When asked how she felt about it, she said: 'Cheated. Cheated. But that was my own fault because I changed my statement'.

Despite the complexity of self-blame and what-ifs, she reflected positively on the whole process:

> *I was terrified. I was sick, physically sick, terrified. But it's the best thing I ever done. Now that it's over, I would say, yeh, that was the right thing to do. I don't know how it would benefit everybody else, I only know I have reached breaking point where I had been pretending or living two separate lives so long.*

Christine did not know that journalists could remain in a closed court. This influenced her to retract part of her statement and the prosecutor accepted a reduced plea so that she would not need to give evidence of sexual abuse. The lack of true anonymity for victims of sexual and intimate partner abuse is increasingly recognised (Tickell, 2020). Reflecting on the impact on sentence was difficult for Christine:

> *that's another thing, that whole waiting between him pleading and sentencing, everything seemed so protracted and drawn out, I couldn't eat, I was going back down weight wise again and I couldn't sleep, I was back to sleeping on the couch and it was just horrible. And then he got 240 hours community service, an 18 month social work supervision order,*

> *3 years non-harassment order and a six month tag.*
> *That was it. So he was out, cock-a-hoop, partying,*
> *but going home in time for his tag.*

Emily supported Christine at court. Having supported many women for whom there was no ultimate disposal or a much lesser sentence, she recognised that this ought to be recognised as a good outcome:

> *she thought he should have gone to jail. How do*
> *you reconcile that? I think it was a good outcome*
> *for what ended up in court, but not for what*
> *actually happened.*

Like Christine, there was a gap between Julie's experience of abuse and the ultimate charges before the court. She initially phoned the police because she believed her life was in danger. When he approached her with a knife – her child in the next room – she struggled with him, grabbed the knife, he struggled to get it back, and was injured in the process:

> *So for eighteen years he abused me, mentally and*
> *physically and he got not even a slap on the wrists –*
> *six months deferred sentence. It just felt like a slap*
> *in the face. And I've got an attempt murder charge*
> *hanging over me. He's got away with this all this time,*
> *I tried to defend myself once and I got an attempt*
> *murder charge and to me, he was just laughing. He*
> *told me for six months leading up to it he was going*
> *to slit my throat so when I saw the knife, that's the*
> *first thing came into my head, he's up to slit my throat.*

Sentencing is based on what was evidenced before the court, but women will perceive the sentence as out of step with their lived experience, compounding feelings of being unheard or not represented.

A GOOD OUTCOME?

In England and Wales, victims of sexual and violent offending have a right to make representations to the probation board on the terms of licence conditions or supervision requirements in the event of release.[12] In Scotland, this right only extends where the offender is serving a life sentence.[13] However, there is a broader right to information when an offender is being released.[14] Nevertheless, errors occur: Jenn was an example when she described being told about her ex-partner's early release a week late. She reflected on what prison meant:

> *The other kind of thing about him being in prison, I wasn't less frightened. I was always less frightened because of the bail conditions. But I felt better knowing that he wasn't anywhere.*

For Jenn, the essence was knowing where he was and the conditions he was subject to, so that she could assess her own safety and the parameters within which she felt secure. This did not resonate with everyone. For Elaine, there was a complex emotional response as she carried guilt for the blame her son attached to his father being in prison:

> *Oh, torture I think is the word. He turned 18 when his dad was in jail. He doesn't want a dad in the jail. It's this police thing, you don't phone the police. So it was back on me. It didn't matter what his dad had done to me in the past, it was my fault.*

Others hoped for a prison sentence that did not come. Within the context of safety fears, still not adequately addressed, this is understandable. Jenn may have been thankful that her safety fears were addressed by a prison sentence, but the delay in reaching that point and the culmination of traumatic waiting and a disconnect from the court process left her deflated despite a 'win'. She explained:

> *And technically we won, that's the whole thing. I phoned Jeannie in Women's Aid and I was like, I wanted to phone you and tell you that he was convicted, like he's properly going to prison, because I don't think that happens very often, it was trying to say to her, look, you won, you have a victory, because I get that for every one of me there must be like fourteen women who just didn't have a whole bunch of people and a whole bunch of luck. It could have been awful, but it was less awful.*

This led Jenn, like many others, to reflect on whether it had been *worth it*.

WAS IT WORTH IT?

Weighing up the costs and benefits of going through with the process is difficult. Having lost her tenancy and faced criminal charges herself, Julie reflected the sentiment of many:

> *I just feel as though I've been let down, it was a waste of time cos I don't know how many times he put a samurai sword to my chest and told me he was going to kill me. I had to leave everything. I just feel let down.*

In both jurisdictions, prosecution is in the public interest and victims can be compelled to attend as witnesses:[15] there is little choice in the matter.[16] Nevertheless, victim engagement underlies a successful prosecution and their testimony remains best evidence. Unsurprisingly, there is a link between victim engagement in the justice process and appropriateness of sentence (Hoyle, 1998). As Megan voiced: 'at the point of sentencing, there's so much more that can be shared'. Thus, it is important to reflect on whether – after the process – women think it was 'worth it'.

Elaine was asked, if she was back in the same situation again, would she call the police. Despite the social pressures within her community and a complex relationship with her own son following the decision to report, she reflected: 'I'd have to. I would have to, but I would be very reluctant'.

Kirsty had a young baby and was still navigating child contact. The charges before the court did not reflect what she reported to the police and potential corroborative evidence was arguably missed. Kirsty had sought independent legal advice, phoned and asked questions, but she still felt frustrated at the end of the process:

> *All the way along, I was like, this is pointless because of the stress. I'm still not sure it was worth all the stress other than it was useful having the bail conditions and the lack of contact.*

Others, however, felt a sisterly duty to prevent the same happening to other women. As Jenn reflected:

> *That was weird. I haven't talked about it in ages. It feels like that's the point of it all. It's not so I can go: this thing happened to me. There has to be something more, that those years can offer the universe, because it's still happening. It's still happening.*

Hannah echoed this sentiment:

> *I don't really tell people much about my experience of court because my experience isn't good. But*

> *I'm very aware that nothing will change if people stop going, but they will stop going. They say more and more women come forward now, but if the outcome is going to be the same as it was, then it'll just go back the way.*

It is important to put these reflections into context. Recall from Chapter Three the women who were exhausted at the first phone call to the police. We witness a shift from a call at a moment of personal crisis to a more general reflection on the need to champion women's safety and protect their children. This is not the picture that is routinely portrayed in the media or even in the courtroom. As Eilidh said: 'I was painted so badly'. Moreover, there is the ongoing safety concern, always gnawing, even if there has been an arguably constructive sentence, as Christine explains:

> *And I have absolutely no doubt in my mind when my three-year non-harassment order is up … that bastard will be sitting at my front gate every single day.*

Within the adversarial process, it is neither feasible nor desirable for individual interests to drive the process: it is a balance of competing views to prove facts and protect the public. Within this environment, there is still scope for victims to be heard and for more to feel that the process has been *worth it*. Victim impact statements (VISs) are a mechanism that ought to bring victims' voices into the process.

VICTIM PERSONAL/IMPACT STATEMENTS

Many common law jurisdictions allow victims the opportunity to give a statement, at the stage of sentencing, on the impact of the crime. VISs were first introduced in the United States in 1976 but did not come to the UK until the early 2000s (Roberts & Manikis, 2012). Victim personal statements (VPSs) were introduced in England and Wales in 2001[17] and VISs were introduced in Scotland in 2003. The VPS in England and Wales is distinct from the VIS in Scotland – and from impact statements in other jurisdictions – because it is designed to inform the *whole* process, not just sentence. The VIS should be taken into account by the prosecutor at the stage of charging. The CPS website provides that the VPS:

> *gives the complainant a voice in the criminal justice process, providing them with an opportunity to explain in their own words how a crime has affected them. For domestic abuse cases, a VPS may also usefully include a complainant's concerns about safety, intimidation and the perpetrator's bail status.*[18]

Guidance on the place of VPSs in the English courts comes from the decision in *R v. Perkins, Bennett and Hall (2013) EWCA Crim 323* which held that, inter alia, the decision to make a statement lies with the victim but once it has been made, it is admitted in evidence and treated as such (i.e. open to cross-examination and challenge). The right to make a statement is reiterated in the Victims' Code (Ministry of Justice, 2020).

A statement ought to be an opportunity for victims to reflect on the impact of the offending against them, relay safety concerns to the court, and provide meaningful insight into the offending to the sentencing judge. They ought to be a good idea. Yet, VPSs have not found high levels of victim satisfaction, despite their promise to lend voice (Sanders & Jones, 2011), largely due to the lack of communication back to victims about how they were used (i.e. the impact of the statement) and due to the false expectations they raise that victim's views will be formative in decision-making.

In Scotland, VISs are distinguishable from their English counterparts as they do not aim to influence sentencing (Chalmers, Duff, & Leverick, 2007). They are limited to certain categories of offences in the High Court and the Sheriff Court sitting as a solemn court.[19] Categories of offending include crimes of violence and sexual offences.[20] Since an evaluation of the pilot phase and their adoption into law,[21] there has been little scrutiny of their application. Early evaluation found high levels of satisfaction in those who chose to make a statement, despite the process being upsetting, but also found relatively low take-up so that the potential benefits of the statements were not fully exploited[22] (Leverick, Chalmers, & Duff, 2007). Research consistently shows low participation across all common law jurisdictions (Roberts & Manikis, 2012): indicators that make a victim more likely to provide a statement include the severity of the offence (Chalmers et al., 2007; Roberts & Manikis, 2012) and domestic abuse victims were not less likely to participate (Hoyle et al., 1998). Since those who provide an impact statement report positively, Roberts and Manikis (2012) surmise that lack of awareness of the opportunity could be a key barrier. Reflecting on domestic abuse, ongoing safety concerns and a lack of faith in the system by the stage of sentencing may also come into play.

In the current research, only Megan was given the opportunity to give an impact statement to the court and that was because her ex-partner died in prison and she gave evidence at a Fatal Accident Inquiry,[23] rather than a criminal trial:

> *I said I wanted to do a statement myself, which I wanted the Sheriff to hear ... I remember the Sheriff at one point looking over at me, he's just looking over at me, as the stuff's being read out, he was starting to understand everything, he was looking like his wig was going to fall off.*

Her vivid description of the judge *getting it*, underlines the impact of being heard and understood. Crucially, she was safe within the court to give this testimony. Even where safety concerns paralyse the process and a statement cannot safely be given prior to sentence, there may be catharsis in being heard.[24] The trial in Canada against Larry Nassar is a good example: Judge Aquilina allowed the victims to be heard, *after* she had sentenced Nassar, former doctor to the United States Gymnastics team, to 40–175 years imprisonment.[25]

Whilst impact statements have the potential to create an opportunity for victims to be heard, they are underused, but the IDVA/IDAA role has increasingly influenced how women engage.

ADVOCACY SERVICES

Supporting women is done in a range of humbling and innovative ways, but advocacy is designed to help women navigate the criminal justice process and make sense of what has happened to them. Jean talks about striving to bridge the gap between expectations and reality: 'no matter what happens, we're still here, we'll still talk to you, just please don't be afraid to call the police again'.

'Success' is subjective, and perceptions of a 'good' outcome will vary. Thus, contextualising decision-making and augmenting victims' voices through advocacy and a more empathic response from criminal justice agencies have the potential to rationalise outcomes and instil greater trust in the process. As Emily observed: 'the bottom line is, it's never going to be easy, no-one's ever going to be happy going to court. Ever'.

The impact of a disappointing sentence was also identified by Jean as a challenge to maintaining women's trust and ensuring their safety and protection in the future:

It's quite dispiriting with the outcomes. But keep reporting because the more you report, then the more that's going on his record and the less likely it is that he'll get admonished and dismissed or whatever. The more likely it is that something will happen to him next time, but that's a skill.

This positive approach to advocacy is important to future safety planning and building trust in the criminal justice response and shows the juxtaposition between the individual and institutional advocacy roles. Megan underscored the importance of IDVAs/IDAAs being physically in the courtroom:

If we are not actually sitting in the court, if we're not actually hearing the reasons why, what's happened in the trial because most of these women give evidence and then disappear and they have no idea what has happened in the body of that trial and how the judge or the jury came to the decision. They don't get any proper feedback.

If advocates are going to translate proceedings and help victims to navigate and make sense of the process, their presence in court seems vital.

CONCLUSION

In the present research, the women who gave evidence and had an 'opportunity' to speak felt no more heard than those women who did not. Views of justice varied, which is consistent with other research (McGlynn et al., 2017). The commonality amongst the research participants was a feeling that not only are decisions unexplained, there is often a lack of clarity around when a decision will be made and the consequences. The process remains blurred which thwarts attempts to regain agency. Resigned despondency was common regardless of the nature of the outcome, suggesting that the way they were treated in the process was more important. Respect, safety, meeting basic needs, and meaningful discussion would arguably improve victim engagement and increase the likelihood of positive case outcomes.

The desire to be heard remains in conflict with pressing safety concerns around going to court, giving evidence, and speaking up. Eilidh suggested that reporting to the police and giving evidence was a risk:

> *It's a huge risk factor. If you're going to put people through the risk factor, if you're going to expose them, you must protect them and not traumatise them in the process with untrained staff and people with no empathy, people with no understanding.*

Whilst the outcome cannot be predictable, it is often more important that women feel heard and respected in the process and that they have contributed to a wider societal response to domestic abuse, than simply treating their own pain. Hannah echoed the SWA's ethos of women-helping-women:

> *Winning wasn't whether the judge found him guilty or anything like that, it was never about a punishment, I always kind of believed that what had happened … but I wanted it on record, to help other people, to help my kids, to help his girlfriend … as much as I was terrified, I was going to keep*

> *the promise I'd made [to myself] and that was that I'd stand there and say what I had to say.*

This underlines the importance of the whole process being perceived fairly and lends weight to the premise that the public interest in prosecuting goes beyond an individual case to the wider endemic problem.

NOTES

1. In England and Wales, sentence can also be suspended. See Sentencing Act 2020, s286.

2. For example, the Caledonia Project in Scotland (Ormston, Mullholland, & Setterfield, 2016) and the Drive Project in England and Wales (www.driveproject.org).

3. High Court in all UK jurisdictions and Crown Court in England and Wales.

4. Magistrates Court, England and Wales.

5. Sheriff Court in Scotland.

6. s35 Sentencing Act 2020, s359 also provides for restraining orders for harassment.

7. Domestic Abuse (Scotland) Act 2018, schedule 1, part I, chapter 4, 9(1) inserts s234AZA into the Criminal Procedure (Scotland) Act 1995.

8. www.sentencingcouncil.org.

9. In both jurisdictions, it is possible to combine a discharge/admonition with a disqualification from driving or an order for compensation.

10. For an understanding of different sentences, see Sentencing Council for England and Wales (www.sentencingcouncil.org) and Scottish Sentencing Council (www.scottishsentencingcouncil.org).

11. Although it is now enshrined in the Victims Code: (i) Scotland: Victims and Witnesses (Scotland) Act 2014, s3B provides for a Victims Code and s3C creates a legislative duty on police to provide victims with a copy of the code and answer reasonable requests for information. (ii) England and Wales: Domestic Violence, Crime and Victims Act 2004, s32 provides for a Victims Code.

12. Domestic Violence, Crime and Victims Act 2004, s35.

13. Victims and Witnesses (Scotland) Act 2014, s28.

14. Victims and Witnesses (Scotland) Act 2014, s27.

15. CPS guidelines describe this as a 'last resort'. Available at: https://www.cps.gov.uk/legal-guidance/domestic-abuse-guidelines-prosecutors.

16. For an insight into the debate on the efficacy of mandatory arrest and pro-prosecution policies, see Hoyle and Sanders (2000) and Buzawa et al. (2017). Critics of the policies argue that they are an infringement of women's agency and choice (Epstein, 1999; Mills, 1998), while proponents identify a link between women's support for mandatory policies and their interactions with police (Coker, 2001; Hanna, 1996).

17. Although there was a Government commitment to them and pilot as early as 1996 (Hoyle, Cape, Morgan & Sanders, 1998).

18. See guidance to prosecutors. Available at: https://www.cps.gov.uk/legal-guidance/victims-and-witnesses-cps-commitments-support.

19. The Victim Statements (Prescribed Courts) (Scotland) Order 2009; there is reference in the *Equally Safe* delivery plan to consultation on extension of the categories (Scottish Government, 2017b).

20. The full list is available in the schedule to the Victim Statements (Prescribed Offences) (Scotland) Order 2009.

21. Criminal Justice (Scotland) Act 2003, s14.

22. A Parliamentary Question to the Scottish Parliament in December 2019 found that in the period 2014–2018, an average of one in six statements were completed.

23. An inquest in England and Wales.

24. The Truth Project in England and Wales and the National Confidential Forum provide examples of safe, confidential environments for victims of non-recent child abuse to talk about their experiences. See www.truthproject.org and www.nationalconfidentialforum.org.

25. https://www.bbc.co.uk/news/world-us-canada-42806911.

Chapter Six

IMPROVING THE JUSTICE RESPONSE

The first two chapters outlined the reforms that have been made to policy and law to tackle GBV, improve victim experiences at court, and address domestic abuse. A triplet of chapters then told the story of women's experiences from a first report to the police to the ultimate conclusion of 'their' case. Why is there such a stubborn misalignment between the policy vision, the legal framework, and women's reality? This chapter explores potential reforms and is in three parts, although procedural justice is at the heart of all the reforms. First, it considers how small, practical changes can make a big difference. Second, it suggests improvements to education and training. Third, it discusses potential reforms through law and policy.

By the end of this chapter you should:

- Understand the concept of procedural justice.

- Appreciate small, tangible shifts throughout the process that can affect positive change.

- Consider the impact of education on undergraduates, professionals, and the judiciary.
- Recognise the impact of different chronologies and be able to situate victim experiences in the current conversation.
- Be aware of the policy and legislative reforms likely to improve victim experiences.

PART I – PROCEDURAL JUSTICE AND PRACTICAL STEPS

What is Procedural Justice?

The underlying premise of procedural justice is that if it is 'fair, inclusive, and respectful' (Rossner, 2017, p. 977), individuals are more likely to obey the law. In essence: 'according to procedural justice theory, the way police officers treat citizens communicates to the latter the extent of their inclusion, value and status within this society' (Bradford, Murphy, & Jackson, 2014). Victims are more engaged if they 'feel that they were treated fairly' (Bell & Nutt, 2012, p. 79), and a positive initial encounter with police reduces victim trauma (Elliot, Thomas, & Ogloff, 2014).

Procedural justice is about the way people interact with formal agencies and how that impacts on their own sense of fairness, inclusion, and perceived value. Procedural justice means recognising that, for most people, going into a police station is scary, attending court is daunting, and the process is alien. Practitioners operate within their *habitus* (Bourdieu, 1987) and do not always pause to think about how they are seen by members of the public: as a representative of a confusing and discomfiting process. Procedural justice acknowledges this and encourages an empathic response. Examples of procedural justice include taking time to explain the process in simple terms; speaking in plain language rather than legal jargon; giving reasons for decisions; recognising that not everyone communicates in the same way and adapting accordingly; using interpreters, interlocutors, supporters, and IDVAs/IDAAs; returning a phone call even if you know you cannot answer the *whys*; and working collegiately with partners. Procedural justice is predicated on a multi-agency response as the process is seen as a whole by members of the public.

Bradford et al. (2014) capture the essence of procedural justice when they describe police officers as mirrors; this underscores the link between procedural justice and recognition of emotions (Murphy, 2014). Karstedt (2014) calls for an emotionally intelligent justice system (see also Tata & Jamieson, 2017). A predominant emotion experienced by many women going through the criminal justice process is fear (Hoyle, 2011; Westmarland, McGlynn, & Humphries, 2018). The empirical data underpinning this book remind us that causes of fear include fear of the perpetrator, fear for their children, and fear of the unknown of the court process. An integral part of the process that impacts on women's response to fear is their expectation of their own role. Here, the need for more transparent police and prosecutorial decision-making comes into sharp focus. If procedural justice is to be met through listening, responding, and communicating, prosecutors need adequate training to distinguish the range of emotions experienced by victims. Often, a victim whom they have dismissed as 'reluctant' could better be understood as fearful. Rather than viewing procedural justice as an add-on, it needs to run through policies. Discretion and decision-making must, especially within domestic abuse prosecution, be understood as a continuum (Hawkins, 2003) if there is to be meaningful procedural justice. Let's explore what that really means.

Moving away from the Punctuation Marks

Policy, practice, and research tend to focus on 'punctuation marks' in the process (Forbes, 2018): a report to the police, providing a statement, trial, and sentence. Yet, the reality is a long, stuttering process where only a minority of cases result in a trial to establish what is proved (Ferguson & McDiarmid, 2014; Green, 2011). There is a tendency to concentrate on key dates in the formal criminal justice process. Each agency, including support services, organises themselves around these key dates. Procedural hearings bear little relevance to a complainer safety planning around the accused's trigger dates, such as birthdays, football games, anniversaries, and Christmas.

When women are asked by the police to answer questions or provide a version of events in the small hours of the morning, in their own home, in the immediate aftermath of a crisis, with no real idea of what will happen next, it is unsurprising that they find the situation stressful. Distracted by the emotional ramifications of what they are experiencing, they do not appreciate that this may be their only opportunity to provide a statement and that there may be no further opportunity to talk about what has happened to them until there is a trial. As Jean observed, the act of reporting to the police begins a process that 'starts to roll and it's unstoppable really', and their choices are constrained.

Often, there is a long unpunctuated gap in communication, as agencies focus on the fixed court hearings; if the trial diet is delayed, so is communication. This is the stage at which GBV policies are applied and efforts are focused on enhanced evidence-gathering, multi-agency working, proactive policing and drafting holistic charges. However, women are often left to wait. The lack of information belies the good intentions of those working hard in the background. Emily summed up:

> *I think women are realistic. They don't expect magic fairy dust. But they do expect to be taken seriously and to be respected and I don't think that's always the case.*

Jumping out of Emily's words is the need to manage expectations. Orientating communication around fixed court dates compounds women's anxiety in waiting, as there are long spells of no communication and misconstrues the likely outcome.

Shifting focus from the trial and looking at the justice response more holistically makes it easier to challenge the power play within a typical domestic abuse prosecution and to address the concerns of the women who perceive a lack of power in the smallest moments of that process. Supporting women through the whole process includes:

- Honest information to victims about the likely length of the case.
- Explaining the whole process and the victim's involvement in it.
- Managing expectations that there might not be a trial and covering different likely outcomes.
- Providing victims an opportunity to give an additional statement.
- Details of how to find out further information.
- Victim-centred communication away from the punctuation marks.
- Advocacy provision should be available to *all* victims of domestic abuse in *all* courts.
- Advocacy provision should be available at the stage of reporting non-recent abuse.

Waiting and the Emotional Response

Chapters Three and Four explored the impact of waiting *for* and *at* court. What is the impact of delay on the court process? There is a need to preserve best evidence and the risk of fading memories. There is, however, a deeper impact. Waiting arguably leads to feelings of institutional disbelief of victim testimony. Within the context of domestic abuse, this predominantly leads to the institutional disbelief of women. Waiting is largely unrecognised and unexamined. The trauma attached to such tense and protracted periods of waiting leads to tertiary victimisation (Forbes, 2018), which goes beyond the secondary victimisation of reporting already recognised (Burman, 2009; Sanders & Jones, 2011).

Propelled into a process they don't understand, women wait for information in a system that focuses on seemingly abstract – and unpredictable – events. All the time, she is scared: scared of his next move, scared for her children, and scared of what will happen at court. Instead of the promised help, reporting to the police creates another unknown, unpredictable fear factor that controls aspects of her life. This is compounded by court delays and is brought into focus for those cases proceeding to trial. After an interminable – and largely misunderstood – wait, the complainer is cited as a witness to court. At the point of trial, there is a shift from being a victim of domestic abuse protected by policy and good intentions to the reality of being a witness in a criminal trial. Despite the protective measures discussed in Chapter Three (e.g. screens, evidence by commissioner, and a support person), the trial remains stressful. The law in England and Wales and in Scotland has long preferred the testimony of the credible and reliable witness who can give a good account of *what happened*. Pause to recall that at the point of the initial report to the police, probably at a point of desperation or crisis, she likely gave a partial story. With advocacy support, there is the possibility that further details are divulged, but lengthy and uncertain waits with things left unsaid cause emotional responses and can impact on women's ability to give evidence. Arriving at court, women feel that this is the culmination of their wait and fear that it will soon be over. Yet, it is just the beginning of another wait but one in which they are fixed in a claustrophobic room, exposed to others' strife, uncomfortable, and terrified. Often, they are asked to go home and come back another day to repeat the process. It is unsurprising that women ultimately present in court as angry, upset, or dissociated.

Where a victim is engaged in the process and it is her advocate's opinion that she will attend court, if required, to give evidence, there should be scope for a standby arrangement. If advocacy services were resourced to provide a safe and therapeutic waiting area, victims and their children could be on standby. The discomfort of the wait could be reduced, even if waiting itself is inevitable. Facilitating more police standby arrangements to reduce the burden on the waiting area would, in the short term, remove a physical barrier, as it would reduce current overcrowding. However, this does not benefit women attending civil court hearings. Long-term, significant revision of court timetabling is needed to reduce time waiting for trial and waiting time at court.

Waiting *for* court could be helped by:

- Court practitioners understanding the impact of waiting and the trauma it causes.

- Tackling the backlog and prioritising domestic abuse cases.

- Being honest with victims about how long they are likely to wait.

- Advocacy support during the wait.

- Contact details of who can advise them on updates when they need them.

Waiting *at* court could be helped by:

- Safe entrances to *all* court buildings.
- Revised expenses rules to ensure fairness to part-time and shift workers.
- Private consultation rooms in all court waiting areas.
- More comfortable waiting areas.
- Increased use of standby arrangements to reduce the number of people waiting.
- Regular updates on what is happening.
- The opportunity to meet the prosecutor.
- Childcare facilities at court.
- Advocacy support at court.

Dealing with Emotion and Recognising Ongoing Abuse

Christie (1986, p. 20) observed that noise does not create good victims and 'needs to be muffled'. This resonates with Eilidh's experience and the pressure to remain calm:

> *There were a few times I had to take a minute. I got very distressed, but probably came across as quite angry under cross-examination continually being called a liar.*

There are two key barriers to being heard. First, the court is retrospective and incident focussed. When the crime has been ongoing for a number of years, several aspects of it seem benign, and if it is ongoing within the courtroom, the law is ill-equipped to cope. Second, societal attitudes to domestic abuse are not as developed as we profess. Most of us would be unsure what to say to someone if we believed that they were a victim of domestic abuse; we would not know what to do to help and we would feel uncomfortable broaching it. That is, if we were perceptive enough to notice in the first place. It is perhaps unsurprising that this is the court response when there is a similar, wider, societal culture.

Recall in Chapters Three–Five the accounts of ongoing abuse despite a report to the police: curries being delivered on each court date, washing line ropes cut, private accounts hacked, stolen gnomes, threats to family members, letters sent to a baby who cannot yet read, 'secrets' to be kept at the child contact centre, allegations made to police of spurious complaints, approaches in the court corridors, and coughing during evidence. These are all examples of behaviour that could seem innocuous or unimportant in isolation but for the women who experienced them and who knew the men, the meaning was clear. They felt threatened and intimidated. This is ongoing abuse during the criminal justice process. Mentioning these 'small' threats, phoning the police about curry deliveries, is what leads to women *feeling crazy*. When family and friends fail to understand, it is unsurprising that women do not report. As Christine explained: 'that's not the perception he gave of himself out with the family' and admitted that when she left him: 'I think they [friends and family] thought it was me that was a bit nuts'.

Domestic abuse is not simply a matter of what happened. Coercive control is a continuum of offending that weaves a complex web. Recall from Chapter 2 that a legal test of reasonableness is applied. In and out of court, the more his reasonableness is tested, the more unreasonable she seems. This leads to women feeling disbelieved at a systemic level and when such feelings can be attributed to structural barriers.

This raises critical questions about how emotions are managed within court and how to address the unpredictable disparity in which voices are heard – and believed – in evidence (M. Davies, 2012; Fitz-Gibbon & Maher, 2015).

Whilst this highlights challenging structural barriers, it hopefully also illustrates the need for national advocacy provision, the impact of waiting not only on individual victims but on the efficacy of the court process, and the importance of time-sensitive and accurate information provision to demystify the process. Societal attitudes to domestic abuse are developing, but it is important to acknowledge enduring stigmas and hidden aspects. The public prosecution of such an inherently private offence is difficult but by always being retrospective and incident focussed, ongoing abuse is 'hidden in plain sight' throughout the court process (P. Davies, 2014).

Ongoing abuse could be challenged by:

- Empathically and appropriately dealing with emotional responses earlier in the process.
- Consistent advocacy provision.
- Minimising the wait.
- Improving timing and means of communication.
- Challenging toxic cross-examination that goes beyond legal questioning.
- Prosecutors better understanding legal aid to help identify financial abuse in the process.

The flaws in the justice system illustrate that the value of advocacy support is thwarted by the broader criminal justice response (Blake Stevenson, 2017). The insensitivity of a police officer, a prosecutor, a bar reporter, a judge, or a solicitor may be dismissed as a 'blip'. However, for each individual who meets such an insensitive approach, the apparent sweep of progress provides little comfort and the whole justice response bears responsibility for her re-victimisation. Without a cultural shift, this picture will not change.

PART II – EDUCATION AND TRAINING

UK government policies (see Chapter One) are committed to improving education on gender inequality and violence against women, particularly to young people still in full-time education. Sexual health education promotes healthy relationships and consent. This is welcome, but the implications of gender inequality need to be woven into the fabric of legal and professional education. Awareness-raising can be stimulated by talking about the everyday impact of gender inequality.

Legal Education

Mary Beard (2017) observed that: 'You can't easily fit women into a structure that is already coded as male; you have to change the structure'. Gender remains a fringe concern, despite defining the whole population. Feminism – and the study of masculinity – is no longer contained to sociology degrees, and the impact of gender inequality imbues an increasingly wider range of study, including law. However, within the law degree, domestic abuse tends to only be seen as relevant to the study of family and criminal law. Even Chapter Two in this book reflects that. To fully recognise the impact of emotional, psychological, and financial aspects of coercive control, domestic abuse needs to be embedded into *all* the core subjects of the degree, including conveyancing, property law, business law, succession, and public law. It is only when it is written into the whole undergraduate degree that there will be meaningful education to future lawyers on the impact of inequality and its relationship with abuse.[1]

Incorporating the impact of gendered violence into the core subjects of the degree is crucial if we are to improve our understanding of economic abuse, appreciate how the law can be used as a tool to perpetrate further abuse, and work towards equal foundations to public policy. By training only our criminal lawyers, we are treating, rather than preventing the problem. An exploration of intersectional inequalities is beyond the scope of this text, but if legal education is to truly reflect the society it serves, we need to do more than write in women and children: lesbian, gay, bisexual, transgender, queer, and intersex (LGBTQI); black minority ethnic (BME); faith; and disability interests are not specialist interests, but they are human interests and ought to be at the core of legal learning.

Professional Training

There is a need to embed and institutionalise domestic abuse training for practitioners. The progress that has been made through accredited programmes like *Domestic Abuse Matters* is just the first step and provision is uneven. It is best understood as awareness-raising training: crucial but an introduction. To make genuine progress, professional training needs to raise awareness and understanding but also work through the practical application within specific roles.

Domestic abuse is a mainstream policing issue yet police training takes a specialist approach, and there is a hierarchy of training. *Domestic Abuse Matters* has been created in consultation with women with lived experience of abuse and understanding the dynamics of offending behaviour is key. However, this is only part of the response. Specialist police officers can understand and recognise offending, but until officers are trauma informed and able to respond appropriately, there is little chance of increased and accurate reporting.

Similarly, prosecutors are trained on the dynamics of domestic abuse but not on how that might translate to their role. The evidential and practical implications of prosecuting abuse go beyond recognising the dynamics. Domestic abuse training should not be treated as an 'add-on' but integrated into basic professional training, including advocacy skills and witness interviewing courses. An empathic prosecutor who takes time to speak to the victim and witnesses ahead of the trial is a good start, but if (s)he does not have the confidence to object to inappropriate cross-examination,[2] an opportunity is lost.

Both judges and prosecutors need to be better versed in risk assessments if they are going to be increasingly used in court. Currently, their understanding of the risk scores has not been tested and training programmes do not go into detail on the risk model. The risk assessment was not developed as a tool for information provision in court, but it is routinely used as such. Often, police provide information in their report to the prosecutor about the relationship and the assessed level of risk. There has been no empirical examination of the weight attached to this information by the prosecutor marking the case; the prosecutor in court; or the judge presiding over the case, if the information is shared by the prosecutor in court. It is unclear if the information is available consistently in all courts and, where it is available, the extent to which it is relied upon. This potentially jeopardises long-term trust in the tool and highlights the need for clarity around its purpose and research on its scientific basis (Ariza, Robinson, & Myhill, 2016). Furthermore, the intrinsic link between the risk assessment and victim advocacy (Robinson & Payton, 2016) means that the way in which advocates have tentatively built trust within the existing court structure is also precarious. There are effectively three professional filters at play: the IDVA/IDAA or police officer conducting the assessment, the prosecutor marking and presenting the case, and the judge adjudicating. The impact of the risk assessment as a tool for court is thus unclear and unpredictable. Not only is this an area where further research is needed, but a better understanding of the questions, scoring, subjectivity, and professional judgement would help prosecutors and judges to apply even weight to the risk score.

The Law Society of Scotland and the Law Society of England and Wales offer training courses on gendered violence in general and domestic abuse in particular. Covid-19 has led to more online training and easier access for many. Beyond the need for continuing professional development (CPD) hours, the courses remain optional. In Scotland, the Lord Justice General, Lord Carloway, has advocated 'ticketing' of solicitors so that they receive an accreditation, like the accreditation currently available to prosecutors, to appear in cases involving domestic abuse (Carloway, 2015). In family courts, there can often be barriers to establishing that domestic abuse has occurred, but such a model of accredited solicitors would be helpful.

Promoting Conversation and Reframing Our Thinking

We read in Chapter One about women gathering in living rooms and community centres to talk about gendered abuse: we saw the impact of a concerted campaign by small pockets of women and the conscious-raising it provoked. Promoting conversation and raising the profile of gender inequality was key to the success of the grassroots effort and led to publications such as The Women's Liberation Movement's magazine *Spare Rib*[3] and the success of media campaign Zero Tolerance: No More Excuses (Mackay, 2001).[4]

Second-wave feminism in the 1970s advanced gender equality and raised awareness of domestic abuse, despite small numbers, no real coherence, little funding, and none of the ways of connecting available today. In a post #MeToo, social media world, the conversation has become more expansive and more inclusive. There are opportunities to experiment, to diversify, and to join a conversation. Of particular relevance to the impact of gender inequality on the legal system and education is the inspiring work of the Feminist Judgements Projects and the charitable contribution of #EmilyTest.

Feminist judgements have been published in England and Wales (Hunter, McGlynn, & Ratcliffe, 2010) and in Scotland (Cowan, Kennedy, & Munro, 2019) as well as several projects worldwide[5] that rewrite published court judgements, adopting the law and evidence of the time, to create an alternative 'feminist judgement'. The project is philosophical, educational, and thought-provoking with a focus on legal decision-making within a reported case (Hunter, 2010). They aim to draft key 'missing' judgements from a feminist vantage point (Fitz-Gibbon & Maher, 2015; Hunter, 2012; Hunter et al, 2010). Both UK projects have addressed domestic abuse: in the English judgements, there was a rewrite of *R v Dhaliwal*[6] to reconfigure suicide after abuse as domestic manslaughter (Burton, 2010; Munro & Shah, 2010); and in Scotland, the judgements have revisited the stalking implications of *HMA v. Drury*[7] (Casey, 2019; McDiarmid, 2019). These rewrites are a novel approach to consciousness-raising of gender blindness within the court process, but they are made more interesting through podcasts, exhibitions, and the way they connect online. They have become more influential than the sum of their parts, and it will be interesting to see how they develop.

In Chapter One, we discussed the influence of family campaigns in victims' names and how they have translated into legal reform. In 2016, Emily Drouet tragically died following an abusive relationship with her boyfriend in the first year of her undergraduate degree. Her parents successfully campaigned to promote research on GBV on university campuses. They have developed a GBV Charter and are calling on universities and colleges to pilot the charter. Their vision is that every higher and further education establishment will pass the 'Emily test' by ensuring prevention, intervention, and support for GBV. This is an ambitious campaign with a ripple effect on educational establishments UK-wide (Drouet & Gerrard-Abbott, 2021) and reflects an identified gap in the conversation.[8]

PART III – POLICY AND LEGISLATIVE DEVELOPMENTS

The Domestic Abuse (Scotland) Act 2018 heralded Scotland as a global leader. It was groundbreaking in criminalising domestic abuse but also in the inclusive approach to drafting the legislation, as the reflections of third-sector agencies were relied upon more than the usual government consultation process (Scott, 2018). Three years later, England and Wales have gone further as the Domestic Abuse Act 2021 not only creates a specific offence, it also concentrates procedural rights for victims in one place and frames them as a step towards greater gender equality within the court process. This is welcome. Both Acts will take time to reach their potential, but the women's narratives in this book suggest supporting reforms in both jurisdictions are needed if the criminality of domestic abuse is to be fully recognised.

There have always been aspects of one jurisdiction learning from the other. The introduction of the Domestic Abuse Act 2021 in England and Wales, following the global recognition of the Domestic Abuse (Scotland) Act 2018 is an obvious example. However, given the success of intermediaries in England and Wales, Northern Ireland, and Australia, it is disappointing that Scotland introduced Evidence by Commissioner in 2019 and did not take the opportunity to extend special measures to include intermediaries.

In Scotland, consideration needs to be given to specific statutory provision, as in England and Wales, to guarantee anonymity. Judicial recommendation that there should be express legislation to guarantee anonymity to complainers in sexual offence trials is welcome (Lady Dorrian, 2021; see also Tickell, 2020) but should extend to all vulnerable victims, including victims of domestic abuse.

Ongoing European Influence

Despite Norway being a continental model, (inquisitorial rather than adversarial) – and increased discourse on the 'Nordic Paradox' (Bjornholt, 2021, p19)[9] – both jurisdictions could adopt the Nordic *Barnehaus* model (Tuveng, 2013) of inclusive, specialist children's centres for children who are victims or witnesses of crime. An evidence review in Scotland recommended its consideration (Carloway, 2015) for children and vulnerable witnesses, and the then Cabinet Secretary for Justice, having visited a similar model in Iceland in 2017, was impressed by the approach (Davidson, 2017). Whilst opportunities have been missed to initiate a *Barnehaus* model in Scotland, it remains on the agenda (Wilson, 2021) with promises of a *Bairns Hoose* by 2025[10] (Wilson, 2021). The charity *Children First* has taken the initiative to create a children's centre on the Nordic model from grant funding that is due to open in 2021. This ought to inspire others. Even without a national policy commitment, local prosecutors could consider greater use of standby arrangements and closer liaison with third-sector agencies so that children and vulnerable witnesses could wait in a more supportive environment and do not need to wait *at* court.

More generally, the development of GREVIO's[11] independent expert reports on the implementation of the Istanbul Convention (Naudi, 2021)[12] offer insights on best practice across Europe, and it is anticipated that there will be valuable recommendations from the pan-European[13] *Improdova* project that is:

> *designed to provide solutions for an integrated response to High Impact Domestic Violence (HIDV), based on comprehensive empirical research of how police and other frontline responders (e.g. medical and social work professionals) respond to domestic violence.*

This is an innovative project that should generate policy from knowledge exchange, highlighting best practice and meshing practitioner experience with research analysis.

Independent Legal Representation (ILR) for Victims

Discussions around ILR for victims have gained popularity since first mooted (Raitt, 2010, 2013). The debate has been influenced by legislative changes that have brought more procedural rights for victims within the adversarial process (see Chapter Two). Inevitably, concerns are raised about fairness to the accused as the rights of both are pitted against one another (Garland, 2001) and victims' rights are ascribed to greater punitivism (Ferguson & McDiarmid, 2014). However, proponents of ILR do not seek representation in substantive aspects of a criminal trial. Instead, they cite successful examples of ILR in Ireland and Canada, where ILR is used only to advise victims on procedural aspects of the case (Raitt, 2013; Taylor, 2019). In Scotland, there have been recent examples of victims seeking ILR to advise on specific procedural aspects of a criminal prosecution, including admissibility of character evidence and whether to invoke the victims' right to review. This has led to a judicial recommendation that publicly funded ILR should be available to all complainers in rape trials, where there is an application to admit sexual history evidence.[14] Yet, whilst the debate is gaining momentum, there is nothing formal in either jurisdiction and no legal aid in place to support such a move (Taylor, 2019). It is anticipated that as the debate gains traction and more test cases are successful, there may be more impetus to fund legal representation. Notwithstanding, EU withdrawal and limited legal aid will continue to make this difficult. Nudging the debate on closer civil/criminal alignment and greater use of the specialist model to promote the best use of the domestic abuse legislation could be a vehicle for reform.

Closer Alignment of the Civil and Criminal Courts

Research has consistently shown the benefit of a specialist criminal justice response to domestic abuse (Burton, 2008; Connelly, 2008; Cook, Burton, Robinson, & Vallely, 2004; Forbes, 2006; Reid Howie, 2007), and this could be strengthened by extending the specialist court remit to adopt a problem-solving model and by extending the breadth of specialism across both jurisdictions. Beyond the scope to improve individual victim's experiences through a more empathic, trained response and to ensure greater accountability in sentencing, specialism is the most effective mechanism to create a closer link between the civil and criminal responses.

The distinction between civil and criminal justice is not recognised by the women who attend court and simultaneously seek to secure a safe child contact arrangement. The women whose stories we read in Chapters Three–Five understood that there were two separate processes and could, in most cases, distinguish between them. However, the practical effect for them was the same: attendance at court. Thus, they broadly considered their whole court experience. In some cases, the civil case was more prominent because of the impact it had on their children's safety. Burton (2008) makes the case for closer integration of the two processes, recognising that for victims, there are often 'blurred boundaries' (p. 128). Indeed, qualitative research with victims of domestic abuse about their experience of attending court and accessing justice consistently illustrates that victims make no distinction between civil and criminal procedure and that two processes, running in tandem, are a potential barrier to justice (Burton, 2008; Cook et al., 2004; Robinson, 2007).

Closer alignment has been described as victims' 'best hope' (Robinson, 2007) of a better interaction with the justice process. Empirical data on an integrated approach are minimal, as there has only been one pilot court within the United Kingdom. Loosely based on the US model (Simon, 2007), its evaluation was tentatively positive (Hester et al., 2008), but there is a need to revisit closer interaction between the two processes. Whilst it was not subject to the same accusations of bias as its US counterpart (Simon, 2007), the sample size was very small (Hester et al., 2008), and the opportunity to understand the full potential of an integrated approach was hampered (Robinson, 2007) by such a narrow data set. Given the limitations – and age – of the pilot, consideration should be given to further pilots. Rather than modelling the US system, a closer relationship between the civil and criminal courts should be tailored to the UK adversarial systems, trauma informed, and built on the foundation of a specialist approach.

The success of a closer integration seems more likely within the framework of a specialist response (Cook et al., 2004). Such a model of coordination and communication is distinct from a blurring or merging of two systems[15] and is mooted within the context of women's narratives which highlight the damaging impact of two potentially concurrent and conflicting court processes offering differing levels of procedural justice, and how that is reflected in their experiences.

A model of closer integration might consider:

- A national advocacy service that is available for both civil and criminal procedure.
- Mutual training and improved communication between civil and criminal practitioners and prosecutors.
- One family/one judge in complex cases – coordinated timetabling.
- Cross-referenced legal aid rules and rules relating to representation.
- Availability of all special measures in civil courts at any hearing women are required to attend, not only at proof.

The fundamental advantage of closer alignment is in its recognition of victims' rights as human rights,[16] as Weisstub (1986) identified:

> *it is in the accommodation of each system to the other that, as legal forms, crime and tort will redress wrongs and meet human needs. (p. 209)*

Weisstub's comments remind us that systems need to complement one another. The current delineation of the criminal and civil court processes is not sustainable if the governments' policy and legislative framework are to be met (victims' right to special protective measures in the criminal court is one example). The legislative intent is not being achieved, and the civil/criminal separation is artificial for families who have experienced domestic abuse.

CONCLUSION

This chapter has discussed a range of proposals to improve the justice response to domestic abuse. It has hopefully shown that there are small steps for students, lecturers, judges, lawyers, prosecutors, police officers, advocacy workers, court clerks, social workers, and bar reporters: everyone has a role in procedural justice. We can all be better, and it only takes a moment to *listen louder*.[17] Moreover, a bigger picture emerges that these steps only make a tangible difference when taken together. The final chapter considers how national advocacy provision, greater specialism, communication through the punctuation marks, and a more informed, empathic approach are all prerequisites for closer alignment of the civil/criminal courts, where there is an opportunity to challenge ongoing abuse, mitigate the impact of waiting, and provide a more just response.

NOTES

1. Further reading available on feminist jurisprudence (Schneider, 2000), feminist prosecutors (Dempsey, 2009), and challenges to

the masculinity of legal doctrine (Schneider, 2000; see also Smart, 1989).

2. See Wheatcroft and Ellison (2012) on the adverse impact of cross-examination.

3. To explore the back catalogue from 1972 to 1993, visit the British Library at https://www.bl.uk/spare-rib#.

4. Available at: https://www.zerotolerance.org.uk/.

5. There have been projects in England and Wales (Hunter et al., 2010), Africa, Australia, Canada, India, New Zealand, and Northern Ireland (Cowan et al., 2019) and a project is developing in Pakistan (@PAKFJP) and Scotland (Cowan et al., 2019). Each project is distinct according to their legal system and the size of their jurisdiction.

6. *R v. Dhaliwal* (2006) EWCA Crim 1139.

7. *Drury v. HMA* (2001) SLT 1013; (2001) SCCR 583. For further discussion, see Chapter One.

8. A report by the National Union of Students in 2013 found that one in four female students reported unwanted sexual behaviour during their time at university/college and one in five experienced sexual harassment in their first week (www.emilytest.co.uk).

9. Despite the high ranking of Nordic countries for their gender equal policies, their reported numbers of domestic abuse remain stubbornly high.

10. This is an SNP manifesto (2017; 2021) commitment that was also part of their Programme for Government (2019) but has yet to be implemented.

11. GREVIO is a group of experts on action against violence against women and domestic violence. It is the independent body responsible for monitoring the implementation of the Istanbul Convention. Available at: www.coe.int.

12. The Istanbul Convention is the Council of Europe Convention on Preventing and Combating Violence Against Women and Domestic Violence (www.coe.int).

13. EU-funded project involving researchers and practitioners from eight countries, Austria, Finland, France, Germany, Hungary, Portugal, Scotland, and Slovenia. Available at: www.improdova.eu.

14. Criminal Procedure (Scotland) Act 1995, s274 prohibits most sexual history evidence (so-called rape shield legislation), but there are exceptions within s275 upon which an application can still be made.

15. For further consideration of legal theory relating to the configuration of the adversarial process and the relationship between the traditional public/private dichotomy, see Duff and Marshall (2010, 2019).

16. Scottish Women's Aid media campaign (SWA, 2017).

Chapter Seven

CONCLUSION

Describing women's experiences of the criminal justice process as behind glass walls acknowledges structural, gendered barriers. In challenging the structure, we must think about an adversarial process that is problematic for all victims, not least those who have experienced domestic abuse. Sanders and Jones (2011) echo Shapland (1986) when they observe that victims are both peripheral and essential to the adversarial trial. They are essential witnesses in the proof of the charge but are still not recognised as a formal party to proceedings, despite being afforded additional rights. It is frequently assumed that the only options are an abolitionist/reform argument (Sanders & Jones, 2011). However, not all the flaws that have been highlighted in this book and elsewhere are attributable to the adversarial process (Hoyano, 2015). This is, literally, academic. The analysis in Chapters One and Two shows a concerted will to improve victims' protection and participation within the existing structures of judicial process, not to compromise those structures. The paradigm of the victim and accused in a 'zero sum game' (Garland, 2001) is an unhelpful misconstruction of the adversarial process. Skolnick (1967, p. 69, in Moody & Tombs, 1982, p. 100) observed that:

> *If the adversary system is defined with only the trial in mind, we are blinding ourselves to the realities of a system of decision-making that is predominantly pre-trial in character.*

Whilst reforms have legitimately been described as 'tinkering' (Walklate, 2004), this book has highlighted meaningful opportunities for victims to be more engaged in the criminal justice process, within the existing adversarial system. Procedural rights and participatory rights[1] are distinguishable, and it is helpful to conceptualise victims' rights as rights which improve a victim's role within the court process and those which support their well-being around the process (Elias, 1986).

The thesis of this book is that the criminal justice response is improved through empathic responses, procedural justice, and shifting the perception that justice is only achieved at trial. First, there is a need to move focus away from the punctuation marks in the process and mitigate the traumatic impact of waiting. Second, the private/public nexus must be seen as a constantly shifting continuum. This has implications for how victims perceive their rights within the process and their expectation of agency and control.

Procedural justice can be achieved by each actor within the process making small changes. However, to realise meaningful change and move beyond glass walls, those steps need to be choreographed by a holistic approach to tackle gender-based violence. In relation to domestic abuse, this is best achieved through consistent national advocacy provision, a specialist – or problem-solving – court response, and closer alignment of the civil and criminal processes.

BETWEEN THE PUNCTUATION MARKS AND MITIGATING THE TRAUMATIC WAIT

Victim focus is rarely on the punctuation marks in the process, but their interaction with criminal justice agencies and support workers is often geared towards key dates. In between, they face long, uncertain waits. This waiting is largely ignored and the impact is under-estimated. The traumatic nature of this unrecognised wait leads to a further, distinct layer of tertiary victimisation (see chapter 6). Victims still describe a situation in which the police remained incident focussed, whilst they struggle to come to terms with long-term abuse. They paint an anxious and alienating experience of court, describing a lack of consistency between the civil and criminal courts, particularly in relation to special measures, and (understandably) question why there is not a more joined-up justice response.

Trying to engage victims on the day of the trial is too late. Attempting to secure best evidence from victims as witnesses in a courtroom is too late. The starting point needs to be much earlier in the process. Waiting times need to be reduced either by greater application of prosecutorial discretion and diversion, so that fewer cases reach court, or through greater resources to facilitate more case preparation and court time. Where waiting is inevitable, it needs to be clearly explained, and a shift is needed to move away from orienting all communication around key decision points. Victims value direct communication with the prosecutor. Expanding provision of advocacy support and encouraging grassroots engagement between the prosecution and IDVAs/IDAAs, there is scope for common understanding and waiting to hold less anxiety. This would dissipate the pressure and anxiety experienced by victims in the build-up to court that is typically under-recognised by criminal justice actors. In fact, there is a great deal that practitioners could contribute to easing some of the pressure by improving communication with victims and their advocates and managing the wait. The current focus on the trial as a byword for the justice response should change.

EVOLVING THE PUBLIC/PRIVATE 'DIVIDE'

The public/private 'divide' is a misconception that fails to recognise the blurred lines between public interests and private lives. This is important for three key reasons. First, it assumes a clear mandate for prosecution in the public interest as a fixed anchor, when it should be seen a constantly shifting continuum of discretion (Hawkins, 2002). Every time a prosecutor reads a file, (s)he should consider the public interest. Thus, whilst there is a *presumption* that prosecution of domestic abuse is in the public interest, if a victim is struggling to engage in the process, it may be appropriate to challenge that presumption and consider the implications of a next time. Second, a public/private dichotomy assumes that reporting private domestic abuse as a crime makes it public and makes it stop. Criminalisation, public prosecution, and robust policies are symbolic of domestic abuse being a social problem that is increasingly tackled in a public forum. There is a sense that it is no longer behind closed doors. However, recognition of a continuum of abuse fails to identify continuing offending alongside and throughout the court process. Women provide numerous examples of sinister, coercively controlling behaviour throughout the court process: during child contact, with the bar reporter, at the police station, in the child welfare hearing, in the corridors of the court, and during the trial. Third, a public criminal justice response to domestic abuse means that the dynamics of abusive behaviour and gendered inequality are duly recognised. Yet it also means that victims, largely female, face the challenge of talking publicly, and in prescribed ways, about intimate aspects of their lives, and there is an expectation about the way in which they should present themselves (Stark, 2007). Within the context of punctuated support, long waits, and unacknowledged ongoing abuse, these are potent barriers to justice. Women's perceptions of the invisibility of the crime (P. Davies, 2014) and the inaudibility of their voice lead to feelings of disengagement and compromise their ability to support the prosecution. Behind glass walls, where abuse is both publicly recognised and privately ongoing, there is a false expectation of victims' rights and agency in the process.

ON AGENCY

The first chapter of this book provides a definition of agency within the court process, as including three key elements: the capacity for informed choice, freedom from further criminal conduct, and a means to be heard. A key challenge remains that there is no actor within the traditional adversarial process whose formal role is to prioritise the interests of the victim. In this context, the role of the victim advocate is to act as a conduit for victims' voices and an assertion of their greater agency (and rights). There is scope for improved communication with criminal justice partners at the micro-level to improve understanding of both the court process and progress in individual cases. In relation to some organisations, this could extend to instilling confidence in them to support women to report to the police and engage with criminal justice partners.

The private control, the public control, and the inner fight for control can be individually conceptualised as layered, yet distinct. It is difficult to conceive of a situation where this could lead to any outcome other than tension. The emotional charge is not easily diluted, and the practical outcome is seemingly irreconcilable positions, pitted against each other.

SMALL STEPS TOWARDS PROCEDURAL JUSTICE

Reflecting on the women's stories you have read, there is no single point at which the process fails, just as no two victims' journeys are the same. Court waiting rooms are overcrowded; sensitive case information is discussed loudly; chairs are uncomfortable; child-care provision is lacking; information provision is slow; rules relating to expenses are inequitable for those who work night shift; and the public areas around the court leave victims feeling vulnerable. Once in the courtroom, the witness box is cramped; there is a requirement to stand for a long time; questions are potentially re-traumatising; the presence of a court reporter causes distress; and there is little objection to cross-examination which goes beyond testing the evidence to an outright attack on character. Having fulfilled a responsibility as a Crown witness, concepts of the 'ideal' victim are reinforced as she is potentially judged to be not sufficiently 'vulnerable' (despite her 'vulnerable' status in law) if she returns to the courtroom to watch the rest of the trial from the public benches. Afterwards, there are unanswered questions. Worryingly, many victims have little understanding of the purpose or effect of the justice response, despite their involvement in it.

An overview of the process distinguishes the seemingly small things. Prosecutors taking a couple of minutes ahead of cases which do proceed to a trial to introduce themselves to the victim and other witnesses is such a small step. Whilst it is intuitive to many, it is not a universal practice. Similarly, making the seats in the waiting area more comfortable, allowing witnesses to be seated giving evidence, and applying the same expenses' rules to day-shift and night-shift workers attending court are quickly achievable. There are also examples of current policy not achieving its aim. For example, witnesses attending court ought to be guaranteed safety, victims should be provided with a clear guide, and the process should be transparent and understandable. These practical measures can make a tangible difference, and they can be done quickly and cheaply. It is in these small shifts in our response to individuals that there is greater hope of engaging victims longer term to have faith and trust in the justice response.

BEYOND GLASSWALLS

There have been manifest policy and legislative changes since the grassroots campaign of second-wave feminism in the 1970s. Chapters One and Two charted the progress which has been made to recognise domestic abuse as a specific offence in law, potentially allowing women to tell the story of their whole lived experience of abuse. Recognition of a continuum of abuse that encompasses emotional, psychological, and financial abuse, rather than focussing on incidents of violence, sets the UK approach apart. It signals a societal understanding of how domestic abuse is perpetrated and a corresponding public condemnation. However, it necessarily remains retrospective. In adducing evidence of criminality, the court process looks back. This shows the complexity and incompleteness of a public criminal justice response to private experiences of domestic abuse that seeks to recognise the dynamics of abusive behaviour and gender inequality. The strength of the Domestic Abuse Act 2021 in England and Wales is its focus on procedural rights. Whilst Scotland has broadly the same legislative provision across different Acts, the consolidation of rights specifically for victims of domestic abuse is a helpful rhetoric in seeking greater procedural justice and sets the scene for a re-conceptualisation of victims' rights as human rights.

Reframing the victim narrative to engage their rights and assist the court to be more attuned to an individual victim's emotional response will not be easy. For many, it may feel uncomfortable. Recognising the continuum and power play in decision-making, understanding the ebb and flow of emotion, challenging the 'ideal' domestic abuse victim, and unpacking the multiple levels between public and private are all critical to realising this approach.

Many victims of domestic abuse will experience both civil and criminal justice procedures. We have seen that they are unlikely to distinguish between them. Connelly (2008) highlighted that closer integration would require significant legislative reform, not least in relation to the burden of proof. However, there are ways in which they might 'accommodate one another'. There is also scope for the infrastructure of advocacy provision to formally provide support through both processes, to provide parity of rights and protection in both courts. In practice, this would be easier to achieve within a specialist structure. Against a backdrop of mitigating waiting times, understanding the dynamics of abuse, providing timely information, and ensuring appropriate outcomes, specialism offers credibility to the legislative intention in both jurisdictions and creates the space for innovative approaches.

The common strand throughout this book is that an empathic response to women's experiences is at the heart of an effective criminal justice response. There are significant gendered barriers to justice for women who have experienced intimate partner and sexual abuse. Yet we have also seen that small steps, taken together and for a shared purpose, can make a big difference to all parties to the justice process.

Conclusion

The process – from phone call, to trial, and beyond – can be fit for purpose. Policy and practice can align and develop coherently. The policy and legislative framework is there to be exploited. Those women who gathered in rooms, established refuges, organised, campaigned, and refused to settle in the 1970s urge us now that 'good' outcomes need not lie forever out of reach. For this, crucially, a commitment to orientate around procedural justice is needed, as we recognise that an empathic response to women's experiences is at the heart of an effective criminal justice response.

NOTE

1. I. Edwards (2004, p. 972) distinguishes between *consultee* or *participator* rights, but his categorisation fails to recognise a simpler right to information, which is better encapsulated by Cape and Ardill's (2004, p. 17) distinction between 'procedural rights' and 'rights of participation'.

REFERENCES[1]

Ariza, J., Robinson, A., & Myhill, A. (2016). Cheaper, faster, better: Expectations and achievements in police risk assessment of domestic abuse. *Policing*, *10*(4), 341–350.

Armstrong, S. (2015). The cell and the corridor: Imprisonment as waiting and waiting as mobile. *Time and Society*, *27*, 133–154.

Ashworth, A. (2014). *Victims' views and the public interest. Criminal Law Review* (editorial).

Ashworth, A., & Zedner, L. (2014). *Preventative justice*. Oxford: OUP.

Baldwin, J., & McConville, M. (1981). *Courts, prosecution and conviction*. Oxford: Clarendon Press.

Barlow, C., Johnson, K., & Walklate, S. (2018). Coercive control cases have doubled – But police still miss patterns of domestic abuse. *The Conversation*, July 23.

Barlow, C., Johnson, K., Walklate, S., & Humphreys, L. (2019). Putting coercive control into practice: Problems and possibilities. *British Journal of Criminology*, *60*(1), 160–179.

Barlow, C., & Walklate, S. (2020). Policing intimate partner violence: The golden thread of discretion. *Policing: A Journal of Policy and Practice*, *14*(2), 404–413.

BBC. (2000). In the shadow of the stalker: Transcript, frontline Scotland. Retrieved from http://news.bbc.co.uk/1/hi/scotland/626002.stm.

BBC News. (2010, May 11). Inside Scotland's only domestic abuse court. Retrieved from http://news.bbc.co.uk/1/hi/scotland/8672758.stm.Accessed on May 11, 2010.

Beard, M. (2017). *Women and power: A manifesto*. London: Profile Books.

Beck, U. (1992). *The risk society: Towards a new modernity*. London: Sage.

Bell, L., & Nutt, L. (2012). Divided loyalties, divided expectations: Research ethics, professional and occupational responsibilities. In T. Miller, M. Birch, M. Mauthner, & J. Jessop (Eds.), *Ethics in qualitative research*. London: Sage.

Bettinson, V. (2016a). Surviving times of austerity: Preserving the specialist domestic violence court. In S. Hilder & V. Bettinson (Eds.), *Domestic violence*. London: Palgrave MacMillan.

Bettinson, V. (2016b). Criminalising coercive control in domestic violence cases: Should Scotland follow the path of England and Wales? *Criminal Law Review*, 3, 165–180.

Bettinson, V., & Bishop, C. (2015). Is the creation of a discrete offence of coercive control necessary to combat domestic violence? *Northern Ireland Legal Quarterly*, 66(2), 179–197.

Bishop, C. (2016a). Why it's so hard to prosecute cases of coercive or controlling behaviour. *The Conversation*, October 31.

Bishop, C. (2016b). Domestic violence: The limitations of a legal response. In S. Hilder & V. Bettinson (Eds.),

References

Introduction: In domestic violence: Interdisciplinary perspectives and intervention. London: Palgrave Macmillan.

Bishop, C., & Bettinson, V. (2017). Evidencing domestic violence, including behaviour that falls under the new offence of 'controlling or coercive behaviour. *The International Journal of Evidence and Proof*, 2017, 1–27.

Bjornholt, M. (2021). Domestic violence and abuse through a feminist lens. In J. Devaney, C. Bradbury-Jones, J. Devaney, R. Macy, C. Øverlien & S. Holt (Eds.), *Routledge international handbook on domestic violence and abuse.* Oxford: Taylor & Francis.

Black, The Right Hon. Justice Lady J., Bridge, J., Bond, T., Gribbin, L. Reardon, M. and Grewcock, P. (2015). *A Practical Approach to Family Law.* OUP.

Blake Stevenson. (2017). *National scoping exercise of advocacy services for victims of violence against women and girls.* Edinburgh: Scottish Government.

Bonomy, L. I. (2015). *The post-corroboration safeguards review, final report.* Edinburgh: Scottish Government.

Bosworth, M., & Kellezi, B. (2017). Doing research in immigration removal centres: Ethics, emotions and impact. *Criminology and Criminal Justice*, 17(2), 121–137.

Bourdieu, P. (1987). The force of law: Toward a sociology of the juridical field. *Hastings Law Journal*, 38(5), 814.

Bradford, B., Murphy, K., & Jackson, J. (2104). Officers as mirrors: Policing, procedural justice and the (re)production of social identity. *British Journal of Criminology*, 54, 527–550.

Brammer, A. & Cooper, P. (2011). Still waiting for a meeting of minds: Child witnesses and family justice systems. *Criminal Law Review*, 12, 925–942.

Breitenbach, E. (2001). The women's movement in Scotland in the 1990s. In E. Breitenbach & F. Mackay (Eds.), *Women and contemporary Scottish politics: An anthology*. Edinburgh: Polygon.

Breitenbach, E., & Mackay, F. (Eds.). (2001). *Women and contemporary Scottish politics: An anthology*. Edinburgh: Polygon.

Brooks, L. (2018). Scotland set to pass "Gold Standard" Domestic Abuse Law. *The Guardian*, February 1. Retrieved from https://www.theguardian.com/society/2018/feb/01/scotland-set-to-pass-gold-standard-domestic-abuse-law.

Brooks, O., & Burman, M. (2015). *Evaluation of support to report pilot advocacy service*. Summary Report Briefing No. 01/2015.

Brooks, O., & Burman, M. (2017). Reporting rape: Victim perspectives on advocacy support in the criminal justice process. *Criminology and Criminal Justice*, 17(2), 209–225.

Brooks, O., & Kyle, D. (2015). *Dual reports of domestic abuse made to the police in Scotland: A summary of findings from a pilot research study*. SIPR Research Summary No. 23.

Brooks-Hay, O. (2018). Policing domestic abuse: The gateway to justice? In O. Brooks-Hay, M. Burman, & C. McFeely (Eds.). *Domestic abuse: Contemporary perspectives and innovative practices*. Edinburgh: Dunedin.

Brooks-Hay, O., Burman, M., & McFeely, C. (Eds.). (2018). *Domestic abuse: Contemporary perspectives and innovative practices*. Edinburgh: Dunedin.

Brown, A. (2016). Scotland's worst domestic abusers unmasked: The monsters who beat and raped more than 65 women. *Daily Record*, December 5.

Browne, S. (2016). *The women's liberation movement in Scotland*. Manchester: Manchester University Press.

Bumiller, K. (2008). *In an abusive state: How neoliberalism appropriated the feminist movement against sexual violence*. Durham, NC: Duke University Press.

Burman, M. (2009). Evidencing sexual assault: Women in the witness box. *Probation Journal*, 56(4), 379–398.

Burman, M. (2018). Domestic abuse: A continuing challenge for criminal justice. In O. Brooks-Hay, M. Burman, & C. McFeely (Eds.). *Domestic abuse: Contemporary perspectives and innovative practices*. Edinburgh: Dunedin.

Burman, M., & Brooks-Hay, O. (2018). Aligning policy and law? The creation of a domestic abuse offence incorporating coercive control. *Criminology and Criminal Justice*, 18(1), 67–83.

Burton, M. (2003, May). Criminalising breaches of civil orders for protection from domestic violence. *Criminal Law Review*, 301.

Burton, M. (2008). *Legal responses to domestic violence*. London: Routledge Cavendish.

Burton, M. (2010). Commentary on R v Dhaliwal. In R. Hunter, C. McGlynn, & E. Rackley (Eds.), *Feminist judgements: From theory to practice* (pps. 255–272). Oxford: Hart.

Burton, M. (2016). A fresh approach to policing domestic violence. In S. Hilder & V. Bettinson (Eds.), *Introduction:*

In domestic violence: Interdisciplinary perspectives and intervention. London: Palgrave Macmillan.

Buzawa, E. S., & Buzawa, A. D. (2013). Evidence-based prosecution: Is it worth the cost? *Criminology and Public Policy*, 12(3), 491.

Buzawa, E. S., Buzawa, C. G., & Stark, E. D. (2017). *Responding to domestic violence: The integration of criminal justice human services* (5th ed.). London: Sage.

CAADA. (2010). *Saving lives, saving money: MARACs and high risk domestic abuse*. Bristol: CAADA Publication. Retrieved from www.safelives.org.

Cape, E., & Ardill, N. (2004). A rebalancing act? *Criminal Justice Matters*, 57(Autumn).

Carloway, L. C. (2011). *The Carloway review: Report and recommendations*. Edinburgh: Scottish Courts Service.

Carloway, L. C. (2015). *Evidence and procedure review*. Edinburgh: Scottish Courts Service.

Casey, J. (2019). Commentary on Drury v HM Advocate. In S. Cowan, C. Kennedy & V. Munro (Eds.), *Scottish Feminist Judgements: (Re)Creating Law from the Outside In*, (pps. 121–125).

Centre for Justice Innovation. (2014). Better courts: A snapshot of domestic violence courts in 2013. Retrieved from http://justiceinnovation.org/wp-content/uploads/2014/03/A-snapshot-of-domestic-violence-courts-2014.pdf.

Centre for Justice Innovation. (2016). Problem-solving courts: An evidence review. Retrieved from http://justiceinnovation.org/wp-content/uploads/2016/08/Problem-solving-courts-An-evidence-review.pdf.

Centre for Justice Innovation. (2017). Problem-solving in Scotland: New developments. Retrieved from http://justiceinnovation.org/wp-content/uploads/2017/09/Problem-solving-in-Scotland-new-development-web.pdf.

Centre for Justice Innovation. (2020). *Time to get it right: Enhancing problem-solving practice in the youth court*. London: Centre for Justice Innovation.

Chalmers, J. (2014). 'Frenzied law making': Overcriminalization by numbers. *Current Legal Problems*, 67(1), 483–502.

Chalmers, J., Duff, A., & Leverick, F. (2007). Victim impact statements: Can work, do work. *Criminal Law Review*, May, 360.

Chalmers, J., & Leverick, F. (2012). Murder through the looking – Glass: Gillon v HM Advocate. *Edinburgh Law Review*, 11(2), 230–236.

Chalmers, J., & Leverick, F. (2013). Scotland: Twice as much criminal law as England? *Edinburgh Law Review*, 17(3), 376–381.

Charles, N., & Mackay, F. (2013). Feminist politics and framing contests: Domestic violence policy in Scotland and Wales. *Critical Social Policy*, 33(4), 593–615.

Christie, N. (1986). An ideal victim. In N. Christie & E. Fattah (Eds.), *From crime policy to victim policy: Re-orientating the justice system*. London: Palgrave Macmillan.

Civil Justice Council. (2020). *Vulnerable witnesses and parties within civil proceedings: Current position and recommendations for change*. London: Courts and Tribunals Judiciary.

Coker, D. (2001). Crime control and feminist law reform in domestic violence law: A critical review. *Buffalo Criminal Law Review*, 4, 801.

Connelly, C. (2008). *Handling domestic abuse cases: A toolkit to aid the development of specialist approaches to cases of domestic abuse.* Edinburgh: Scottish Government.

Connelly, C. (2011). Specialist responses to domestic abuse. In H. Hughes (Ed.), *Domestic abuse and scots law.* Edinburgh, Greens.

Connelly, C., & Cavanagh, K. (2007, December). Domestic abuse, civil protection orders and the 'new criminologies': Is there any value in engaging with the law? *Feminist Legal Studies, 15*(3), 259–287.

Cook, D., Burton, M., Robinson, A., & Vallely, C. (2004). *Evaluation of specialist domestic violence courts/fast track systems.* London: Home Office.

Cooper, P., & Mattison, M. (2017). Intermediaries, vulnerable people and the quality of evidence: An international comparison of three versions of the English intermediary model. *The International Journal of Evidence and Proof, 21*(4), 351–370.

Coppel, J. Q. C. (2018). *Opinion on the European Union (Withdrawal) Bill – E.U. Charter of Fundamental Rights.* Equality and Human Rights Commission. Retrieved from www.equalityhumanrights.com.

Cowan, S., Kennedy, C., & Munro, V. (2017, December). *Scottish feminist judgements project. SCOLAG, 482.*

Cowan, S., Kennedy, C., & Munro, V. (Eds.). (2019). *Scottish feminist judgements: (re)Creating law from the outside in.* Oxford: Hart.

Crawford, A., & Goodey, J. (Eds.). (2000). *Integrating a victim perspective within criminal justice: International debates.* Aldershot: Dartmouth Publishing Company.

Croal, H. (2005). Criminal justice in the devolved Scotland. In G. Mooney & G. Scott (Eds.), *Exploring social policy in the 'new' Scotland*. Cambridge: Polity Press.

Crown Office. (2018). Prosecution code. Retrieved from http://www.copfs.gov.uk/images/Documents/Prosecution_Policy_Guidance/Prosecution20Code20_Final20180412__1.pdf.

Crown Prosecution Service. (2013). *Code for crown prosecutors* (7th ed.). London: Crown Prosecution Service.

Crown Prosecution Service. (2020). *Domestic abuse guidelines for prosecutors*. The Crown Prosecution Service. Retrieved from www.cps.gov.uk.

Cuthbert, J., & Irving, L. (2001). Women's aid in Scotland: Purity versus pragmatism? In E. Breitenbach & F. Mackay (Eds.), *Women and contemporary Scottish politics: An anthology*. Edinburgh: Polygon.

Davidson, J. (2017). *Interview: Michael Matheson on an evidence-led approach to justice*. Edinburgh: Holyrood. Retrieved from https://www.holyrood.com/articles/news/domestic-violence-rehabilitation-programme-be-expanded-across-scotland.

Davies, M. (2012). The law becomes us: Rediscovering judgement. *Feminist Legal Studies*, 20(2), 167–181.

Davies, P. (2011a). *Gender, crime and victimisation*. London: Sage.

Davies, P. (2011b). Lessons from the gender agenda. In S. Walklate (Ed.), *Handbook of victims and victimology*. London: Routledge.

Davies, P. (2014). Gender first: The secret to revealing sexual crimes and victimisation. In P. Davies, P. Francis, & T. Wyatt (Eds.), *Invisible crimes and social harms*. London: Palgrave.

Dempsey, M. (2009). *Prosecuting domestic violence: A philosophical analysis*. Oxford: OUP.

Devaney, J., Bradbury-Jones, C., Macy, R., Øverlien, C., & Holt, S. (Eds.). (2021). *Routledge international handbook on domestic violence and abuse*. Oxford: Taylor & Francis.

Di Rollo, A. (2017). Keynote address by Alison Di Rollo, QC, Solicitor General for Scotland. *Scottish Women's Aid Conference*, Edinburgh, December 1.

Dickson, A., Jackson, A., Laing, I., & Rosengard, A. (2010). The use and effectiveness of exclusion orders under the Matrimonial Homes (Family Protection) (Scotland) Act 1981. In *Preventing homelessness*. Scottish Women's Aid Research Report.

Dobash, R. E., & Dobash, R. P. (1979). *Violence against wives: A case against the patriarchy*. London: Macmillan.

Dorrian, Rt Hon. Lady, L., Lord Justice Clerk. (2021). *Improving the management of sexual offences cases: Final report from the Lord Justice Clerk's Review Group*. SCTS. Retrieved from www.scotcourts.gov.uk.

Douglas, H. (2018). Legal systems abuse and coercive control. *Criminology and Criminal Justice*, *18*(1), 84–99.

Drouet, F. M. B. E., & Gerrard-Abbott, P. (2021). *Response to consultation feedback: EmilyTest Gender Based Violence Charter*. Retrieved from www.emilytest.co.uk.

Duff, R. A., & Marshall, S. E. (2010). Public and private wrongs. In J. Chalmers & F. Leverick (Eds.), *Essays in memory of Sir Gerald Gordon*. Edinburgh: Edinburgh University Press.

Duff, R. A., & Marshall, S. E. (2019). Crimes, public wrongs and civil order. *Criminal Law and Philosophy*, *13*(1), 27–48.

References

Duggan, M. (Ed.). (2018). *Revisiting the ideal victim: Developments in critical criminology*. Bristol: Policy Press.

Dunn, J. L., & Powell-Williams, M. (2007). Everybody makes choices: Victim advocates and the social construction of battered women's victimization and agency. *Violence Against Women, 13*(10), 977–1001.

Edwards, I. (2004). An ambiguous participant: The crime victim and criminal justice decision-making. *British Journal of Criminology, 44*, 967–982.

Edwards, S. (1989). *Policing domestic violence*. London: Sage.

Elias, R. (1986). Community control, criminal justice and victim services. In N. Christie & E. Fattah (Eds.), *From crime policy to victim policy: Reorienting the justice system*. London: Palgrave Macmillan.

Elliot, I., Thomas, S., & Ogloff, J. (2014). Procedural justice in victim-police interactions and victims' recovery from victimisation experiences. *Policing and Society, 24*(5), 588–601.

Epstein, D. (1999). Effective intervention in domestic violence cases: Rethinking the roles of prosecutors, judges and the court system. *Yale Journal of Law and Feminism, 11*, 3–50.

Fenwick, H. (1997). Procedural rights of victims of crime: Public or private ordering of the criminal justice process. *Modern Law Review, 60*(3), 317.

Ferguson, P. R., & McDiarmid, C. (2014). *Scots criminal law: A critical analysis* (2nd ed.). Edinburgh: Edinburgh University Press.

Fielding, A. (2018). The phrase that changed feminism. *Stylist*, June.

Fitz-Gibbon, K., & Maher, J. (2015). Feminist challenges to the constraints of law: Donning uncomfortable robes? *Feminist Legal Studies*, *23*, 253–271.

Fitz-Gibbon, K., & Walklate, S. (2017). The efficacy of Clare's law in domestic violence law reform in England and Wales. *Criminology and Criminal Justice*, *17*(3), 284–300.

Forbes, E. (as Provan). (2006, December). Abuse in the system. *Journal of the Law Society of Scotland*. Retrieved from http://www.journalonline.co.uk/Magazine/51-12/1003677.aspx.

Forbes, E. (2010). Family joy as date set for 40CDO marines' return. *BBC News*. Retrieved from www.news.bbc.co.uk/local/somerset/hi/people_and_places/newsid_9006000/9006621.stm.

Forbes, E. (2018). The Domestic Abuse (Scotland) Act 2018: *The whole story? Edinburgh Law Review*, *22*, 406–411.

Foster, R. (2016). Doing the wait: An exploration into the waiting experiences of prisoners' families. *Time and Society*, *28*(2), 459–477.

Gadd, D. (2017). Domestic violence. In A. Liebling, S. Maruna, & L. McAra (Eds.), *The Oxford handbook of criminology* (6th ed.). Oxford: OUP.

Garland, D. (2001). *The culture of control: Crime and social order in contemporary society*. Oxford: OUP.

Gillan, A. (2014). Scotland's got it right on domestic abuse: It takes it seriously. *The Guardian*, March 27. Retrieved from https://www.theguardian.com/commentisfree/2014/mar/27/scotland-domestic-abuse-british-police-forces.

Gold, A. (2021) *Protecting Vulnerable Parties and Witnesses in Civil Proceedings*. Lexology online retrieved at: Protecting vulnerable parties and witnesses in civil proceedings - Lexology.

Gondolf, E. W. (2010). The contributions of Ellen Pence to batterer programming. *Violence Against Women, 16*(9), 992–1006.

Gondolf, E. W., & Fisher, E. R. (1988). *Battered women as survivors: An alternative to treating learned helplessness*. Washington, DC: Lexington Books.

Graham, H., & McIvor, G. (2015). *Scottish and international review of the uses of electronic monitoring*. Scottish Centre for Crime and Justice Research Report 8/15.

Graham, H., & McIvor, G. (2017). Advancing electronic monitoring in Scotland: Understanding the influences of localism and professional ideologies. *European Journal of Probation, 9*(1), 62–79.

Green, S. (2011). Crime, victimisation and vulnerability. In S. Walklate (Ed.), *Handbook of victims and victimology*. London: Routledge.

Greenan, L. (2004). *Violence against women: A literature review*. Edinburgh: Scottish Executive.

Grierson, J. (2018). Council funding for women's refuges cut by nearly £7m since 2010. *The Guardian*, March 23. Retrieved from https://www.theguardian.com/society/2018/mar/23/council-funding-womens-refuges-cut-since-2010-england-wales-scotland.

Hanmer, J., & Itzin, C. (Eds.). *Home truths about domestic violence: Feminist influences on policy and practice, a reader*. London: Routledge.

Hanna, C. (1996). No right to choose: Mandated victim participation in domestic violence prosecutions. *Harvard Law Review*, *109*, 1849.

Hanna, C. (2009). The paradox of progress: Translating Evan Stark's coercive control into legal doctrine for abused women. *Violence Against Women*, *15*(12), 1458–1476.

Hawkins, K. (2002). *Law as last resort: Prosecution decision-making in a regulatory agency*. Oxford: OUP.

Hawkins, K. (2003). Order, rationality and silence: Some reflections on criminal justice decision-making. In L. Gelsthorpe & N. Padfield (Eds.), *Exercising discretion: Decision-making in the criminal justice system and beyond*. London: Willan.

Herman, J. (2001). *Trauma and recovery: From domestic abuse to political terror*. Philippines: Pandora.

Hester, M. (2013). Who does what to whom? Gender and domestic violence perpetrators in English police records. *European Journal of Criminology*, *10*(5), 623–637.

HM Government. (2016). *Violence against women and girls strategy, 2016–2020*. London: Home Office.

HMCPSI and HMICFRS. (2020). *Evidence led domestic abuse prosecutions*. London: Home Office.

HMIC. (2014). *Everyone's business: Improving the police response to domestic abuse*. London: Home Office.

HMICS. (1997). Hitting home: Thematic inspection on domestic abuse. Edinburgh: Scottish Executive.

HMICS. (2008). *Thematic inspection on domestic abuse*. Edinburgh: Scottish Government.

Home Office (2005; *updated 2021) Code for Victims*. London: Home Office.

Home Office. (2013). *Domestic violence and abuse: A new definition*. London: Home Office.

Home Office. (2015). *Controlling of coercive behaviour in an intimate or family relationship: Statutory guidance framework*. London: Home Office.

Howarth, E., & Robinson, A. (2016). Responding effectively to women experiencing severe abuse: Identifying key components of a British advocacy intervention. *Violence Against Women, 22*(1), 41–63.

Hoyano, L. (2015). Reforming the adversarial trial for vulnerable witnesses and defendants. *Criminal Law Review, 107*, 115–119.

Hoyle, C. (1998). *Negotiating domestic violence: Police, criminal justice and victims*. Oxford: OUP.

Hoyle, C. (2000). Being a bloody nosey cow: Ethical and methodological issues in researching domestic violence. In R. King & E. Wincup (Eds.), *Doing research on crime and justice*. Oxford: OUP.

Hoyle, C. (2011). Feminism, victimology and domestic violence. In S. Walklate (Ed.), *Handbook of victims and victimology*. London: Routledge.

Hoyle, C. (2012). Victims, victimisation and restorative justice. In M. Maguire, R. Morgan, & R. Reiner (Eds.), *The Oxford handbook of criminology*. Oxford: OUP.

Hoyle, C., Cape, E., Morgan, R., & Sanders, A. (1998). *Evaluation of the one-stop shop and victim statement pilot projects*. London: Home Office.

Hoyle, C., & Palmer, N. (2014). Family justice centres: A model for empowerment. *International Review of Victimology*, 20, 191.

Hoyle, C., & Sanders, A. (2000). Police responses to domestic violence: From victim choice to victim empowerment? *British Journal of Criminology*, 40, 14–36.

Hughes, H. (Ed.). (2011). *Domestic abuse and Scots law*. Edinburgh: Green.

Hunter, R. (2010). An account of feminist judging. In R. Hunter, C. McGlynn, & E. Rackley (Eds.), *Feminist judgements: From theory to practice* (pp. 30–43). Oxford: Hart.

Hunter, R. (2012). The power of feminist judgements? *Feminist Legal Studies*, 20, 135–148.

Hunter, R., McGlynn, C., & Rackley, E. (Eds.). (2010). *Feminist judgements: From theory to practice*. Oxford: Hart.

Itzin, C. (2000). The criminal justice response to women who kill: An interview with Helena Kennedy Q.C. In J. Hanmer & C. Itzin (Eds.), *Home truths about domestic violence*. London: Routledge.

Jackson, J., & Summers, S. (2012). *The internationalisation of criminal evidence: Beyond the common law and civil law traditions*. Cambridge: Cambridge University Press.

Johnson, M. P. (2008). *A typology of domestic violence: Intimate terrorism, violent resistance, and situational couple violence*. Boston, MA: North Eastern University Press.

Karstedt, S. (2014). *Handle with care: Emotions, crime and justice*. In S. Karstedt, I. Loader, & H. Strang (Eds.), *Emotions, Crime and Justice*. Oxford: Hart.

Kelly, L. (1987). The continuum of sexual violence. In J. Hanmer & M. Maynard (Eds.), *Women, violence and social control*. London: Palgrave Macmillan.

Kelly, L. (1988). *Surviving sexual violence*. Cambridge: Polity Press.

Kelly, L., Loveatt, J., & Regan, L. (2005). *A gap or a chasm? Attrition in reported rape cases*. London: Home Office Research Study.

Lacey, N., & Zedner, L. (2017). Criminalization: Historical, legal and criminological perspectives. In A. Liebling, S. Maruna, & L. McAra (Eds.), *The Oxford handbook of criminology* (6th ed.). Oxford: OUP.

Lavalette, M., & Mooney, G. (1999). New Labour, new moralism: The welfare politics and ideology of New Labour under Blair. *International Socialism Journal, 85*, 27–47.

Leverick, F., Chalmers, J., & Duff, P. (2007). *The pilot victim statement schemes in Scotland*. Project Report, Scottish Executive, Edinburgh.

Lombard, N. (2018). *The Routledge handbook of gender and violence*. London: Routledge.

Lombard, N., & MacMillan, L. (2013). *Violence against women: Current theory and practice in domestic abuse, sexual violence and exploitation*. London: Jessica Kingsley.

Mackay, F. (2001). The case of zero tolerance: Women's politics in action? In E. Breitenbach & F. Mackay (Eds.), *Women and contemporary Scottish politics: An anthology*. Edinburgh: Polygon.

Mackay, F. (2010). Gendering constitutional change and policy outcomes: Substantive representation and domestic violence policy in Scotland. *Policy and Politics*, *38*(3), 369–388.

Marr, A. (2008). *A history of modern Britain*. London: Pan.

Matczak, A., Hatzidimitriadou, E., & Lindsay, J. (2011). *Review of domestic violence policies in England and Wales*. London: Kingston University and St George's University of London.

McAra, L. (2008). Crime, criminology and criminal Justice in Scotland. *European Journal of Criminology*, *5*(4), 1477–3708.

McDiarmid, C. (2019). Judgement on Drury v HM Advocate. In S. Cowan, C. Kennedy & V. Munro (Eds.). *Scottish Feminist Judgements: (Re)Creating Law from the Outside In* (pps. 109–120).

McDiarmid, C. (2019). Reflective Statement on Drury v HM Advocate. In In S. Cowan, C. Kennedy & V. Munro (Eds.), *Scottish Feminist Judgements: (Re)Creating Law from the Outside In* (pps. 126–130).

McFeely, C. (2016). *The health visitor response to domestic abuse*. Unpublished Ph.D. thesis, University of Glasgow, Glasgow.

McGlynn, C., Rackley, E., & Houghton, R. (2017). Beyond 'revenge porn': The continuum of image-based sexual abuse. *Feminist Legal Studies*, *25*(1), 25–46.

McMillan, L. (2015). The role of the specially trained officer in rape and sexual offence cases. *Policing and Society*, *25*(6), 622–640.

Mills, L. G. (1998). Mandatory arrest and prosecution policies for domestic violence: A critical literature review and the case for more research to test victim empowerment. *Criminal Justice and Behaviour*, 25(3), 306–318.

Ministry of Justice. (2020). *Code of practice for victims of crime in England and Wales*. London: Crown Copyright.

Mlambo-Ngcuka, P. (2020). *Violence against women and girls: The shadow pandemic*. New York, NY: UN Women.

Monckton-Smith, J. (2021). *In control: Dangerous relationships and how they end in murder*. London: Bloomsbury.

Monckton-Smith, J., Williams, A., & Mullane, F. (2014). *Domestic abuse, homicide and gender: Strategies for policy and practice*. Cham: Springer.

Moody, S., & Tombs, J. (1982). *Prosecution in the public interest*. Edinburgh: Scottish Academic Press.

Mooney, G., & Scott, G. (2005). Introduction. In G. Mooney & G. Scott (Eds.), *Exploring social policy in the 'new' Scotland*. Cambridge: Polity Press.

Munro, V., & Shah, S. (2010). R v Dhaliwal: Reconstructing manslaughter in cases of domestic violence suicide'. In R. Hunter, C. McGlynn, & E. Rackley (Eds.), *Feminist judgements: From theory to practice* (pp. 261–272). Oxford: Hart.

Murphy, K. (2014). Procedural justice, emotions and resistance to authority. In S. Karstedt, I. Loader, & H. Strang (Eds.), *Emotions, crime and justice*. Oxford: Hart.

Myhill, A., & Hohl, K. (2016). The 'golden thread': Coercive control and risk assessment for domestic violence. *Journal of Interpersonal Violence*, 34(21–22), 4477–4497.

Myhill, A., & Johnson, K. (2016). Police use of discretion in response to domestic violence. *Criminology and Criminal Justice*, 16(1), 3–20.

Mythen, G. (2011). Cultural victimology: Are we all victims now? In S. Walklate (Ed.), *Handbook of victims and victimology*. London: Routledge.

Naudi, M. (2021). Foreword. In J. Devaney, C. Bradbury-Jones, R. Macy, C. Øverlien & S. Holt (Eds.), *Routledge international handbook on domestic violence and abuse*. Oxford: Taylor & Francis.

Nichols, A. J. (2014). No-drop prosecution in domestic violence cases: Survivor-defined and social change approaches to victim advocacy. *Journal of Interpersonal Violence*, 29(11), 2114–2142.

Oliver, R., Alexander, B., Roe, S., & Wlasny, M. (2019). *The economic and social costs of domestic abuse: Research report 107*. London: Home Office.

Ontiveros, M. (2005). Rosa Lopez, David Letterman, Christopher Darden and Me: Issues of gender, ethnicity and class in evaluating witness credibility. *Hastings Women's Law Journal*, 6, article 2.

Ormston, R., Mullholland, C., & Setterfield, L. (2016). *Caledonia system evaluation: Analysis of a programme for tackling domestic abuse in Scotland*. Edinburgh: Opsi Mori and Scottish Government.

Packer, H. L. (1964). Two models of the criminal process. *University of Pennsylvania Law Review*, 113(1).

Phillips, R., Kelly, L., & Westmarland, N. (2013). *Domestic violence perpetrator programmes: An historical overview*.

Discussion Paper. London Metropolitan University and University of Durham.

Pizzey, E. (1974). *Scream quietly or the neighbours will hear*. New York, NY: Penguin.

Police Scotland and COPFS. (revised 2017). *Joint protocol between Police Scotland and the Crown Office and Procurator Fiscal Service: In partnership challenging domestic abuse*. Edinburgh: Police Scotland and COPFS.

Raitt, F. (2010). *Independent legal representation for complainers in sexual offence trials*. Glasgow: Rape Crisis Scotland.

Raitt, F. (2013). Independent legal representation in rape cases: Meeting the justice deficit in adversarial proceedings. *Criminal Law Review*, 9, 729.

Reid Howie. (2007). *Evaluation of the pilot domestic abuse court*. Edinburgh: Scottish Executive.

Renzetti, C. (2013). *Feminist criminology*. London: Routledge.

Roberts, J., & Manikis, M. (2012). Victim personal statements: Latest (and last) trends from the witnesses and victims experience survey in England and Wales. *Criminology and Criminal Justice*, 13(3), 245–261.

Robinson, A. (2006a). *Advice, support, safety and information services together (ASSIST): The benefits of providing assistance to victims of domestic abuse in Glasgow*. Cardiff: Cardiff University.

Robinson, A. (2006b). Reducing repeat victimisation among high-risk victims of domestic violence: The benefits of a coordinated community response in Cardiff, *Wales. Violence Against Women, 12*(8), 761–788.

Robinson, A. (2007). Improving the civil–criminal interface for victims of domestic violence. *The Howard Journal of Criminal Justice, 46*(4), 356–371.

Robinson, A. (2017a). Serial domestic abuse in Wales: An exploratory study into its definition, prevalence, correlates, and management. *Victims and Offenders, 12*(5), 643–662.

Robinson, A. (2017b). *Establishing the efficacy of a telephone-based police response to domestic abuse: Hampshire constabulary's resolution centre. Final Report*, Crime and Security Research Institute.

Robinson, A., & Clancy, A. (2015). *Development of the priority perpetrator identification tool (PPTI) for domestic abuse: Final report*. Cardiff: Cardiff University.

Robinson, A., & Clancy, A. (2020). Systematically identifying and prioritising domestic abuse perpetrators for targeted intervention. *Criminology and Criminal Justice*.

Robinson, A., & Howarth, E. (2012). Judging risk: Determinants in British domestic violence cases. *Journal of Interpersonal Violence, 27*(8), 1489–1518.

Robinson, A., & Hudson, K. J. (2011). Different yet complementary: Two approaches to supporting victims of sexual violence in the UK. *Criminology and Criminal Justice, 11*(5), 515–533.

Robinson, A., Myhill, A., & Wire, J. (2018). Practitioner (mis)understandings of coercive control in England and Wales. *Criminology and Criminal Justice, 18*(1), 1–21.

Robinson, A., & Payton, J. (2016). Independent advocacy and multi-agency responses to domestic violence. In S. Hilder & V. Bettinson (Eds.), *Introduction: In domestic violence: Interdisciplinary perspectives and intervention*. London: Palgrave Macmillan.

Robinson, A., Pinchevsky, G. M., & Guthrie, J. A. (2016). Under the radar: Policing non-violent domestic abuse in the U.S. & U.K. *International Journal of Comparative and Applied Criminal Justice, 40*(3), 195–208.

Robinson, A., & Rowlands, J. (2009). Assessing and managing risk among different victims of domestic abuse: Limits of a generic model of risk assessment. *Security Journal, 22*(3), 190–204.

Robinson, A., & Tregidga, J. (2007). The perceptions of high-risk victims of domestic violence to a coordinated community response in Cardiff, *Wales. Violence Against Women, 13*, 1130–1148.

Rock, P. (2004). *Constructing victims' rights: The Home Office and New Labour*. Oxford: OUP.

Rock, P. (2011). Theoretical perspectives on victimisation. In S. Walklate (Ed.), *Handbook of victims and victimology*. London: Routledge.

Rossner, M. (2017). Restorative justice in the twenty-first century: Making emotions mainstream. In A. Leibling, S. Maruna, & L. McAra (Eds.), *The Oxford handbook of criminology* (6th ed.). Oxford: OUP.

Rotter, R. (2016). Waiting in the asylum determination process: Just an empty interlude? *Time and Society, 25*(1), 80–101.

Rowlands, J. (2019). *Reviewing domestic homicide: International practice and perspectives*. Churchill Fellowship

Paper. Winston Churchill Memorial Trust. Retrieved from www.wcmt.org.uk.

Rummery, K. (2013). Partnership working and tackling violence against women: Pitfalls and possibilities. In N. Lombard & L. MacMillan (Eds.), *Violence against women: Current theory and practice domestic abuse, sexual violence and exploitation*. London: Jessica Kingsley.

SafeLives. (2021). The domestic abuse bill – Migrant children and their families joint briefing: Report stage (Lords). Retrieved from https://safelives.org.uk/sites/default/files/resources/Domestic%20Abuse%20Bill%20Report%20Stage%20%28Lords%29%208th%20March%202021.pdf.

Sanders, A., & Jones, I. (2011). The victim in court. In S. Walklate (Ed.), *Handbook of victims and victimology*. London: Routledge.

Schneider, E. (2000). *Battered women and feminist lawmaking*. London: Yale University Press.

Scott, M. (2018). Foreword: It's different in Scotland. In O. Brooks-Hay, M. Burman, & C. McFeely (Eds.), *Domestic abuse: Contemporary perspectives and innovative practices*. Edinburgh: Dunedin.

Scottish Executive. (2000, November). *National strategy to address domestic abuse in Scotland*. Edinburgh: Scottish Partnership on Domestic Abuse.

Scottish Executive. (2003). *A national strategy for the prevention of domestic abuse*. Edinburgh: Scottish Executive.

Scottish Government. (2009). *Safer lives: Changed lives: A shared approach to tackling violence against women in Scotland*. Edinburgh: The Scottish Government and COSLA.

Scottish Government. (2010). *What does gender have to do with violence against women?* Edinburgh: Scottish Government.

Scottish Government. (2015, updated 2020). *Code for victims.* Edinburgh: Scottish Government.

Scottish Government. (2016). *Equally safe: Scotland's strategy for preventing and eradicating violence against women and girls – Update.* Edinburgh: Scottish Government.

Scottish Government. (2017a). *National scoping exercise of advocacy services for victims of violence against women and girls.* Edinburgh: Scottish Government.

Scottish Government. (2017b). *Equally safe delivery plan.* Edinburgh: Scottish Government.

Scottish Government. (2018). *Equally Safe: Scotland's Strategy to prevent and eradicate violence against women and girls.* Edinburgh: Scottish Government.

Scottish Women's Aid. (2017). *Speaking out: Recalling Women's Aid in Scotland, 40 years of Scottish Women's Aid.* Edinburgh: Scottish Government.

Shapland, J. (1986). Victims and the criminal justice system. In N. Christie & E. A. Fattah (Eds.), *From crime policy to victim policy.* London: Palgrave Macmillan.

Shaw, A. (2020). *Supporting survivors of domestic abuse: Early findings from the third sector.* Scotland in Lockdown Report. Scotland in Lockdown.

Sheehy, E. (2018). Expert evidence on coercive control in support of self-defence: The trial of Teresa Craig. *Criminology and Criminal Justice, 8*(1), 100–114.

Shepard, M. F., & Pence, E. (1999). *Coordinating community responses to domestic violence: Lessons from Duluth and beyond.* London: Sage.

Sherman, L. W., & Berk, R. A. (1984). The specific deterrent effects of arrest for domestic assault. *United States of American Sociological Review, 49,* 261–272.

Simon, J. (2007). *Governing through crime.* Oxford: OUP.

Stanko, E. (2000). Victims R Us. In T. Hope & R. Sparks (Eds.), *Crime, risk and insecurity.* London: Routledge.

Stanko, E. (2001). The day to count: Reflections on a methodology to raise awareness about the impact of domestic violence in the UK. *Criminal Justice, 1*(2), 215–226.

Stark, E. (2007). *Coercive control: The entrapment of women in personal life.* Oxford: OUP.

Strickland, P. (2012). Labour Policy on Domestic Violence – 1999-2010. *House of Commons Library, retrieved at: Standard Note (parliament.uk).*

Sutherland, E. (2018). The welfare test: Determining the indeterminate. *Edinburgh Law Review, 22*(1), 94.

Tata, C., & Jamieson, F. (2017, April). Just emotions? The need for emotionally-intelligent justice policy. *Scottish Justice Matters, 5*(1), 32–33.

Taylor, L. (2014). The English and Welsh perspective on legal aid for crime victims. In P. Wiliński & P. Karlik (Eds.), *Improving protection of victims' rights: Access to legal aid.* Sofia: CSD.

Taylor, L. (2019). *Independent legal representation for crime victims.* Open Justice.

Taylor-Dunn, H. (2016). The impact on victim advocacy on the prosecution of domestic violence offences – Lessons from a realistic evaluation. *Criminology and Criminal Justice*, *16*(1), 21–39.

Thomson, J. (2014). *Family law in Scotland* (7th ed.). London: Bloomsbury.

Thomson, L. (2017). *Review into victim care in the justice sector in Scotland*. Edinburgh: Crown Office.

Tickell, A. (2020). Why don't sexual offence complainers have a right to anonymity in Scotland? *Edinburgh Law Review*, *24*(3), 427–434.

Tolmie, J. R. (2017). Coercive control: To criminalize or not to criminalize? *Criminology and Criminal Justice*, *18*(1), 1–17.

Towers, J., & Walby, S. (2012). *Measuring the impact of cuts in public expenditure on the provision of services to prevent violence against women and girls*. Report for Northern Rock Foundation and Trust for London.

Turnbull, S. (2016). 'Stuck in the middle': Waiting and uncertainty in immigration detention. *Time and Society*, *25*(1), 61–79.

Tuveng, M. R. (2013). *That is children's right – Is not it? How does Statens Barnehus bring forward children's rights to be heard?* Master's thesis, Norwegian University of Science and Technology, Trondheim.

Walby, S., & Myhill, A. (2000). *Reducing domestic violence ... what works? Assessing and managing the risk of domestic violence. Policing and Reducing Crime Briefing Note, Crime Reduction Research Series*, University of Leeds, Leeds.

Walby, S., & Towers, J. (2018). Untangling the concept of coercive control: Theorizing domestic violent crime. *Criminology and Criminal Justice*, *18*(1), 7–28.

Walby, S., Towers, J., & Francis, B. (2016). Is violent crime increasing or decreasing? A new methodology to measure repeat attacks making visible the significance of gender and domestic relations. *British Journal of Criminology*, *56*, 1203–1234.

Walker, L. (1979). *The battered woman*. Manhattan, NY: Harper and Row.

Walklate, S. (2011). Perspectives on the victim and victimisation. In S. Walklate (Ed.), *Handbook on victims and victimology*. London: Routledge.

Walklate, S., & Fitz-Gibbon, K. (2021). Why criminalise coercive control? The complicity of the criminal law in punishing women through furthering the power of the state. *International Journal for Crime, Justice and Social Democracy*, *9*(4).

Walklate, S., Fitz-Gibbon, K., & McCulloch, J. (2018). Is more law the answer? Seeking justice for victims of intimate partner violence through reform of legal categories. *Criminology and Criminal Justice*, *18*(1), 115–131.

Walklate, S., & Mythen, G. (2011). Beyond risk theory. *Criminology and Criminal Justice*, *11*(2), 99–113.

Weisstub, D. (1986). Victims of crime in the criminal justice system and Epilogue on the rights of victims. In N. Christie & E. Fattah (Eds.), *From crime policy to victim policy: Reorienting the justice system*. London: Palgrave Macmillan.

Westmarland, N. (2015). *Violence against women: Criminological perspectives on men's violence*. London: Routledge.

Westmarland, N., Johnson, K., & McGlynn, C. (2017). Under the radar: The widespread use of 'out of court resolutions' in policing domestic violence and abuse in the United Kingdom. *British Journal of Criminology, 58*(1), 1–16.

Wheatcroft, J. M., & Ellison, L. E. (2012). Evidence in court: Witness preparation and cross-examination style effects on adult witness accuracy. *Behavioural Sciences and the Law, 30,* 821–840.

Whitecross, R. (2017). Section 11 orders and the "abuse" provisions: Family lawyers' experience and understanding of section 11(7A)-(7E). *Edinburgh Law Review, 21,* 269.

Whyte, R. (2016). *Open letter to mark the 30th anniversary of rape crisis*. Unpublished. University of Glasgow, Glasgow.

Williams, L., & Walklate, S. (2020). Policy responses to domestic violence, the criminalisation thesis and 'learning from history'. *The Howard Journal of Crime and Justice, 59*(3), 305–316.

Wilson, L. (2021). SNP pledge to create 'Bairn's Hoose' for child victims of crime. *Holyrood Magazine*, April 5.

Zedner, L. (2002). Victims. In M. Maguire, R. Morgan, & R. Reiner (Eds.), *The Oxford handbook of criminology* (3rd ed.). Oxford: OUP.

Zydervelt, S., Zajac, R., Kaladelfos, A., & Westera, N. (2016). Lawyers' strategies for cross-examining rape complainants: Have we moved beyond the 1950s? *British Journal of Criminology, 57*(3), 551–569.

EU/UN Charters, Conventions and Directives:

Charter of Fundamental Rights of the European Union, 2000.
Council of Europe Convention on Preventing and Combating Violence Against Women and Domestic Violence, Istanbul, 2011.
European Union Directive on Victims' Rights, 2012.
United Nations Convention on the Elimination of All Forms of Discrimination Against Women (CEDAW), 1979.

UK Legislation

Abusive Behaviour and Sexual Harm (Scotland) Act 2016.
Children (Scotland) Act 1995.
Children (Scotland) Act 2020.
Civil Partnership Act 2004.
Civil Procedure Act 1997.
Civil Procedure (Amendment) Rules 2021.
Criminal Justice (Scotland) Act 2003
Criminal Law (Consolidation) (Scotland) Act 2010.
Criminal Practice Direction 2013.
Domestic Abuse Act 2021.
Domestic Abuse (Protection) (Scotland) Act 2021.
Domestic Abuse (Scotland) Act 2011.
Domestic Abuse (Scotland) Act 2018.
Domestic Violence, Crime and Victims Act 2004.
European Union (Withdrawal) Act 2018.
Family Law Act 1996.
Family Law (Scotland) Act 2006.
Freedom of Information (Scotland) Act 2002.
Matrimonial Homes Act 1983.

Matrimonial Homes (Family Protection)(Scotland) Act 1981.
Practice Direction 1A.
Practice Direction (CA (Crim Div): Criminal Proceedings: General Matters) (2013) EWCA Crim 1631; cemented in law by the Criminal Procedure Rules 2015.
Protection from Abuse (Scotland) Act 2001.
Protection from Harassment Act 1997.
Sentencing Act 2020.
Serious Crime Act 2015.
Supreme Court Act 1981.
Victims and Witnesses (Scotland) Act 2014.
Vulnerable Witnesses (Criminal Evidence) (Scotland) Act 2019.
Youth Justice Criminal Evidence Act 1999.

Case Law

Drury v. HMA 2001 SLT 1013; 2001 SCCR 583.
LRK against AG (2021) SAC (civ) 1.
Opuz v. Turkey Application no. 33401/02, 09/06/09.
Procurator Fiscal Hamilton against John Donnelly (2021) SAC (Crim) 2.
R v. Dhaliwal, 2006 EWCA Crim 1139.
Re W (2010) UKSC 12.

NOTE

1. This is an abridged reading list. A full bibliography is available at: British Library EThOS: Perception and reality : an exploration of domestic abuse victims' experiences of the criminal justice process in Scotland (bl.uk)

INDEX

Note: Page numbers followed by "*n*" indicate notes.

Abusive behaviour, 52
Adversarial process, 137
Adversary system, 174
Advocacy, 26
    individual, 25
    institutional, 25
    services, 140–141
    support, 80–83
Agency, 7–8, 91–95, 177–178
Anti-climax and realisation of fears, 127–129

Batterer intervention program, 23
Beijing Platform for Action, 20–21
Black minority ethnic (BME), 158
Blair New Labour administration, 21
British Crime Survey, 9

Charter of Fundamental Human Rights of the European Union, 21

Children (Scotland) Act 1995, 55
Children First, 163
Civil Justice Council, 49, 66*n*16
Civil Law (*see also* Criminal Law)
    in England and Wales, 47–49
    in Scotland, 54–57
Civil Partnership Act 2004, 55
Civil Procedure (Amendment) Rules 2021, 48–49
Civil remedy, 60–61
Clare's Law, 31–32
Closer alignment of civil and criminal courts, 165–168
Coercive control, 16, 59, 155
    throughout court process, 113–118
Communitarian approach, 22

Community-based disposal, 124
Concurrent civil proceedings, impact of, 110–113
Continuing professional development (CPD), 160
Conversation and reframing thinking, 160–162
'Conveyer-belt' court, 23
Coordinated Action Against Domestic Abuse (CAADA), 41n14
Counting Dead Women database, 34
Court, 99–100, 123
  advocacy services, 140–141
  anti-climax and realisation of fears, 127–129
  being sent home, 104–106
  coercive control throughout court process, 113–118
  impact of concurrent civil proceedings, 110–113
  culture, 107
  evidence, 107–110
  feeling unheard, 126–127
  good outcome, 134–135
  lived experience, 131–134
  personnel assume waiting, 101
  possible outcomes, 124–126
  prosecution, 135
  provision of information, 130
  VISs, 137–140
  waiting at court, 101–104
Covid-19 global pandemic, 63
Crime survey, 10
Criminal courts, 101
Criminal Injuries Compensation Authority (CICA), 40n4, 47
Criminal Justice and Licensing (Scotland) Act 2010, 33
Criminal justice process, 173
Criminal Law
  in England and Wales, 50–54
  in Scotland, 56–60
Criminal Law (Consolidation) (Scotland) Act 2010, 58
Criminal Practice Direction, 50
Criminalisation thesis, 61–63

Index

Crown Office and Procurator Fiscal Service (COPFS), 6, 27
Crown Prosecution Service (CPS), 6, 36
Custody court, 1

Dash Risk Checklist, 28, 41*n*16
Disclosure Scheme for Domestic Abuse Scotland (DSDAS), 31
Domestic Abuse (Scotland) Act 2011, 55
Domestic Abuse (Scotland) Act 2018, 56–59, 62, 162–163
Domestic abuse, 5–6, 11–12, 21, 158–159
  nature and scale of, 8–9
Domestic Abuse Act 2020, 58
Domestic Abuse Act 2021, 6, 50, 59, 124, 163, 179
Domestic Abuse Best Practice Framework, 36
Domestic Abuse Bill, 52
Domestic Abuse Matters, 27, 158
Domestic Abuse Pilot Court, 2
Domestic Abuse Protection Notices/Orders, 60
Domestic Abuse Task Force in Scotland, 29
Domestic homicide review (DHR), 34
Domestic Violence Crimes and Victims Act 2004, 34, 48, 50
Domestic Violence Liaison Officers, 19
Domestic Violence Protection Notices (DVPNs), 30
Domestic Violence Protection Orders (DVPOs), 30–31
Duluth model, 22–23

Education, 157–162
  legal, 157–158
  professional, 157–158
#EmilyTest, 33
Emotion and recognizing ongoing abuse, 154–157
Emotional response, 152–154
Empathy (justice response), 89, 118, 142
Engender, 20
English civil law, 46
English criminal law, 46
Equality and Human Rights Commission, 21
Equally Safe, 37–39
  delivery plan, 35
EU (Withdrawal) Act 2018, 63

European Convention on Human Rights (ECHR), 21
European influence, 163–164
European Union (EU), 19, 46
Evidence, 107–110

Family campaigns, 32–34
Family Law Act 1996, 48
Feminism, 11–12, 157
Feminist judgements, 161
Financial penalty, 125
Funding, 22, 83

Gender (approach; barriers; policies), 17, 173
Gender equality, 12
Gender-based violence (GBV), 33, 162
Gendered policies, 35
  Equally Safe, 37–39
  Violence Against Women and Girls Strategy, 2016–2020, 36–37
Glasgow Sheriff Court, 1
Glasgow Women's Liberation group, 17
Glass ceiling, 4
Glass Walls, 4–5, 179–181
Grassroots, consciousness-raising from, 17–19
GREVIO development, 164

High Impact Domestic Violence (HIDV), 164
HMA v. Drury, 161
Home Office, 18
Homicide Reviews, 34–35
Human Rights Act 1998, 21

Ideal victim, 107
Imprisonment, 124
Improdova project, 164
Independent Domestic Abuse Advocates (IDAAs), 25, 80, 83
Independent Domestic Violence Advocates (IDVAs), 25
Independent Legal Representation (ILR), 164–165
Individual advocacy, 25
Institutional advocacy, 25
Intermediaries, 50–51, 163
Istanbul Convention, 35, 47

Judicial training, 28
Jurisdictions, 35
Justice for Women, 20
Justice process, 86–87
Justice response, 147
  education and training, 157–162
  policy and legislative developments, 162–168
  procedural justice, 148–157

Index

Law, 45
  civil remedy, 60–61
  criminalisation thesis, 61–63
  current challenges, 63–65
  UN and EU influence, 46–60
Law Society of England and Wales, 160
Law Society of Scotland, 160
Legal education, 157–158
Lesbian, gay, bisexual, transgender, queer, and intersex (LGBTQI), 158

Matrimonial Homes (Family Protection) (Scotland) Act 1981, 54
Matrimonial Homes Act 1983, 47
Megan's Law, 32
Mixed-method approach, 10
Multi-agency approach, 22–35
Multi-agency conferences, 28–30
Multi-Agency Public Protection Arrangements (MAPPA), 29
Multi-agency response, 16, 64, 126, 149
Multi-agency risk assessment conference (MARAC), 28–29, 81

National Code of Practice, 18
National crime surveys, 9
National Delivery Group, 36
National Strategy to Address Domestic Abuse in Scotland, 22
New Labour government, 22
New Labour manifesto (1997), 21
Nonharassment order (NHO), 55, 58, 123–124
Nordic *Barnehaus* model, 163
Nordic Paradox, 163

Our Call to End Violence Against Women and Girls, 36

Party litigants, 49
Perceptions of justice, 123
Perpetrator programmes, 36, 124
Pilot victimisation study, 9
Police assessing risk, 84–87
Police response, 15–16, 20, 73, 75–76, 79–80
Police Scotland, 6, 9
Policy and legislative developments, 162
  closer alignment of civil and criminal courts, 165–168
  European influence, 163–164
  ILR, 164–165

Policy approach, 15
  consciousness-raising from Grassroots, 17–19
  gendered policies, 35–39
  multi-agency approach and risk model, 22–35
  victims' rights, 19–22
Practice Direction 1A, 49
Problem-solving courts, 24–25
Procedural justice, 148, 174
  emotion and recognizing ongoing abuse, 154–157
  punctuation marks, 150–151
  small steps, 178–179
  waiting and emotional response, 152–154
Professional education, 157–158
Professional training, 158–160
Prosecution, 135
Prosecutors, 159
Protection from Abuse (Scotland) Act 2001, 55
Protection from Harassment Act 1997, 48, 55, 57–58
Protective measures, 47–50, 56, 58, 60–61, 101, 112
Provision of information, 130

Public interest, 176
Public/private 'divide', 176–177
Public/private nexus, 2
Punctuation marks, 150–151, 175–176

R v *Dhaliwal*, 161
Re W (2010) UKSC 12, 49
Reasonableness, 52, 155
Reclaim the Night march, 18, 117
Refuge provision, 54
Risk assessments, 28–30, 80–83
Risk indicator checklist (RIC), 27, 41n16
Risk model, 22–35
Rough sex defence, 53

SafeLives, 26–28, 54, 80, 82
Safety planning, 17, 26, 80, 87, 141, 150
Sarah's Law, 31–32
Scottish civil law, 46
Scottish Crime and Justice Survey, 9
Scottish criminal law, 46
Scottish Women's Aid (SWA), 2, 9
Scream Quietly or the Neighbours Will Hear, 17
Second-wave feminism, 161
Sentencing, 133–134
Serious Crime Act 2015, 51

Index

Service rights, 20
Social work reports, 124
Spare Rib (Women's Liberation Movement's magazine), 161
Special measures, 49, 163, 167, 175 (*see also* Protective measures)
Specialist courts, 23–25

Tertiary victimization, 152, 175
Thatcher government, 19
Training, 27–28, 157–162
Traumatic wait, 175–176
Trial, 51, 60, 73–74, 91, 101, 104, 106–107

UK government policies, 157
UK-wide policies, 35
UN Convention on the Elimination of Discrimination Against Women and girls (CEDAW), 13*n*4
UN Declaration on Violence Against Women, 20

Victim Charter for England and Wales, 20
Victim impact statements (VISs), 137–140
Victim personal statements (VPSs), 137–140
Victim Support, 2, 18, 20
Victims, 2, 6, 148
　advocacy support and risk assessments, 80–83
　advocates, 25–27
　agency, 91–95
　empowerment model, 7
　experience before court, 73
　ideal, 107
　implications of waiting, 89–90
　interest, 132
　named laws, 32
　police assessing risk, 84–87
　reporting to police, 75–80
　rights, 19–22
　survivors, 6
　waiting for court, 87–89
Victims and Witnesses (Scotland) Act, 47, 58, 59
Violence Against Women and Girls Strategy (VAWG Strategy), 6, 36–37
Vulnerable persons database (VPD), 33

Waiting, 152–154
　for court, 87–89
　at court, 101–104
　implications of, 89–90

Witness Service, 2
'Women-Helping-Women-Helping-Women', 10
Women's Aid Federation for England (WAFE), 17

Youth Justice Criminal Evidence Act 1999, 51

Zero sum game, 173–174

www.ingramcontent.com/pod-product-compliance
Lightning Source LLC
Chambersburg PA
CBHW071408300426
44114CB00016B/2225